THE OX AND THE SLAVE:
A SATIRICAL MUSIC DRAMA IN BRAZIL

THE OX AND THE SLAVE:
A SATIRICAL MUSIC DRAMA
IN BRAZIL

a new and revised introduction

by

KAZADI wa MUKUNA

DIASPORIC AFRICA PRESS, INC.

*In the memory of my father Mukuna Simon
and my mother Kabena Astrid Helene*

This book is a publication of

Diasporic Africa Press

New York | www.dafricapress.com

Copyright © Diasporic Africa Press 2016

Revised and updated edition

All rights reserved. No part of this publication may be reproduced or distributed in any form or by any means, or stored in a database or retrieval system, without the prior written permission of the publisher.

Library of Congress Control Number: 2015956287

ISBN-13 978-1-937306-37-3 (pbk.: alk paper)

CONTENTS

Acknowledgements i

Preface iii

Introduction to the First Edition vii

Introduction to the Second Edition xvii

CHAPTER I

An Argument for the Brazilian Origin of Bumba-meu-boi 1

CHAPTER II

Structural Organization of Bumba-meu-Boi 23

CHAPTER III

Sotaque: Styles and Stylistic Changes 71

CHAPTER IV

The Assimilation of Bumba-meu-Boi in Maranhão 97

CHAPTER V

Anatomy of Bumba-meu-Boi Song Texts 109

Conclusion 125

Appendix 1 129

Appendix 2 145

Glossary 183

Bibliography 191

Notes 203

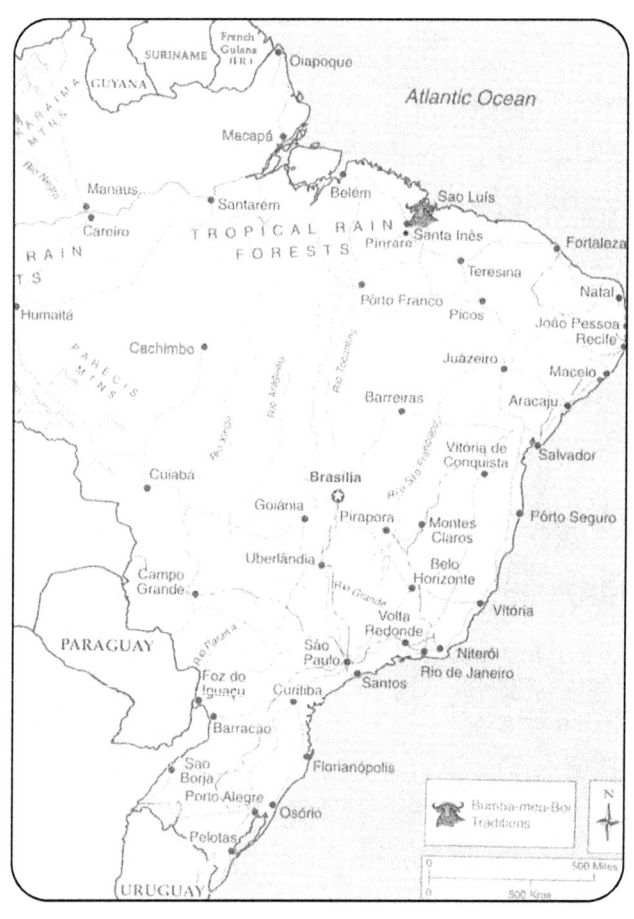

Map of Brazil

ACKNOWLEDGEMENTS

I owe debts of gratitude to so many friends, American and Brazilian, that it is impossible to give all their names here. Nevertheless, I must thank my student Leonel Marins at the Federal University of Maranhão who in 1981 made it possible for me to gain a closer look of the Bumba-meu-Boi by introducing me to Mr. José Vale, the leader of the Rei da União troupe in Pindaré Mirim. My gratitude goes to Mr. and Ms. José Vale, Mr. Manuel Gaiola, and the entire troupe in Pindaré for their explanations of the Bumba-meu-Boi. I am grateful to Maria de Rosário Campos for her dedication and continuous assistance during the preliminary research trips to Pindaré, São Inez and Bacabal. The process of lyric transcription, translation, and clarification would have been impossible without her explanation of the hidden meanings of the metaphors, which only a native of Maranhão could understand.

My sincere gratitude goes to Cynthia Zaldokas for reading preliminary drafts of this book and to Marguerite Goral for gladly spending so much of her time editing versions of this project to the final format. I thank my friend, colleague and brother Gerhard Kubik for taking a moment from his crazy schedule to read this manuscript and provide valuable comments. My gratitude goes to Jean Campos and Alain-Laurent Campos Kazadi for their assistance in further data gathering (filming and taping) during the 2000 statewide celebration of Bumba-meu-Boi in São Luis. I am grateful to the Earthwatch Foundation for providing two teams of American volunteers who donated their time and money to support the data-collecting phase of the project in summer of 1986. I am also grateful to the Brazilian government through its branch Conselho Nacional de Desenvolvimento Científico e Tecnológico – CNPq for the grant which permitted me in 2000 to verify data for this project in the field. I must thank Mr. Jomar Moraes, then the Secretary of Culture of the state of Maranhão, for partially financing the project in São Luis.

I am grateful to Kevin Alexander Wilson for his assistance with the music illustrations. Finally yet importantly, I am also grateful to the filmmaker and friend Bill Oliver for donating his talent and time to film the drama. My heartfelt thanks go to the artist C. Warren Cullon for donating the original watercolor painting used on the cover of this book.

PREFACE

In the words of the well known saying among Brazilian social scientists: *O Brasil não é para principiantes* (Brazil is not for beginners).[1] The same can be said about Bumba-meu-Boi. This Brazilian topic is difficult to decipher by a novice who is unfamiliar with this culture or has not studied deeply the principles of its popular music. In these terms, Kazadi wa Mukuna is not a beginner. For more than two decades, his book entitled *Contribuição Bantu na Música Popular Brasileira* (Bantu Contribution to the Popular Music of Brazil [Global Editora, 1979]) remained a classic among students of Latin American culture in general and those of Africanisms in Brazil in particular. The popularity of this study encouraged another publisher to reprint a new version entitled *Contribuição Bantu na Música Popular Brasileira: Perspectivas Etnomusicológicas* (*Bantu Contribution to the Popular Music of Brazil: Ethnomusicological Perspectives* [Terceira Margem, 2000]). Today this monumental work continues to be sought and cited by scholars and nonprofessionals alike.

Kazadi initiated his work on Bumba-meu-Boi in the 1980s. When I edited *Einführung in Musiktraditionen Brasiliens* (1986), a collection of articles devoted to Brazilian music, I included the first version of Bumba-meu-Boi articles "Bumba-meu-Boi in Maranhão" by Kazadi. Reviewers of this collection pointed out then the unique analytical line of focus Kazadi had applied to his study. Since then, much has been published by various authors on the subject, but none has been capable of duplicating the thinking mind of Kazadi, which is continuously seeking new insights to analyze a cultural manifestation such as Bumba-meu-Boi. *A brincadeira mais linda* (the most beautiful merrymaking), as it is known by its participants, the performance of Bumba-meu-Boi is simultaneously a symbolic universe rich in scenic recourses and a vast and fertile field of ethnomusicological research.

In this research, Kazadi has addressed more than the questions of methodology. He has reformulated a series of incomplete or even misleading concepts nurtured and fostered by various writers about this folk drama in the state of Maranhão. He provides an up-to-date and a comprehensive study of Bumba-meu-Boi in Maranhão with an unprecedented detailed interpretation. With this study, Kazadi has contributed to the demystification of this fascinating folk drama, and shed light on a significant segment of the Brazilian popular culture. By applying a multidisciplinary method and theory to this study, he has constructed a model for the ethnomusicological study. Kazadi has demonstrated to us in a very convincing manner that in the cultural field there exist a thin semantic line between the concepts of innovation and creation. This conceptual aspect has been ignored by scholars, as evidenced in the bibliography of the existing literature on the subject. Here Kazadi has revealed the value of an interdisciplinary research by bringing together anthropology, history, linguistic, musicology, semantics and sociology, capable of producing a rich result on the subject.

In addition, the reader has finally a stimulating research tool that transcends the interdisciplinary approach of Bumba-meu-Boi and discusses the true focus of an ethnomusicological study. With this work, the author confirms the historical origins of the folk drama is of less concern for ethnomusicologist, but rather understanding of its semantic structure as a linguistic, scenic and musical perspective, beyond the performance as content of social vindication and worldview, in search of the truth of Bumba-meu-Boi. Kazadi's interpretation of the Bumba-meu-Boi provides an analytical model for all who will study this folk drama in the near future.

The conclusion that one reaches after reading this study is that Bumba meu Boi is a conceptualized form that is continuously renovated to guarantee its continuity as a resilient cultural manifestation that adapts itself to socio-cultural demands of the societies where its participants live. This conclusion permeates beyond the explication of Bumba-meu-Boi. It opens a window on an important period of Brazilian history and sheds light on an aspect of Brazilian culture and its popular manifestations, which has come together in different styles of controversial elements, thus creating a scenic culture of incalculable wealth. With *The Ox and the Slave*, Kazadi wa Mukuna has proved to us Brazilians that he is not a beginner and that we still have plenty to learn from him.

—Prof. Dr. Tiago de Oliveira Pinto
University of São Paulo

INTRODUCTION TO THE FIRST EDITION

My first contact with Bumba-meu-Boi was in 1976 when I visited São Luis, Maranhão, on a research trip to double check data for a project. On that occasion, I became empathetic with the music and the drama of this cultural manifestation about which I understood nothing. Although I was investigating another subject, I thought I would talk with some participants and staff members at the *Fundação Cultural do Maranhão* (Cultural Foundation of Maranhão), and read up on the subject in local libraries. It was not until 1980, while teaching at the *Universidade Federal do Maranhão* (Federal University of Maranhão) in São Luis, that I began an intensive investigation of Bumba-meu-Boi, devoting most of my fieldwork energy to collecting information from various troupes in the area and compiling bibliographic references.

On May 21, 1981, I made my first field trip to Pindaré, a small town situated on the main land, about 259 kilometers south of the capital island of São Luis. My students at the university boasted about the city of Pindaré as having one of the most authentic versions of Bumba-meu-Boi. The agenda for the following day included meetings with Dona Maria and Senhor Manoel Gaiola, members of *Boi de Zé Vale*, one of the two Bumba-meu-Boi troupes in the area. This year the troupe had selected *Rei da União* (King of the Union) as the theme for their ox. The reception was very warm and everyone was anxious to explain all about their *brincadeira mais linda* (the most beautiful merrymaking).

Later that day I met Mr. Armando, president of the troupe, who lives on a ranch where all the rehearsals are held. It is on this ranch that the first and the last performances, respectively known as the *Nacimento de Boi* (Birth of the Ox) and the *Matança de Boi* (Killing of the Ox) are enacted. I was able to see and photograph the troupe's entire instrumentation as well as the ox and its various *lombos* (hides) from the previous year, which were being used this year for rehearsals.

That evening I met Mr. José Vale, Dona Maria's husband and the owner of the troupe who also plays the role of *Amo* (Master) in the play. Mr. Vale has his colleagues' respect as the most knowledgeable person in the community about Bumba-meu-Boi. He proved this to me during our meeting with explanations that were extremely detailed and comprehensible. I was particularly impressed by the manner in which he explained the "Killing of the Ox" section of the drama with illustrations. Members of his family and his daughter, Dalvanira de Jesus Vale, who plays the role of indigenous chief in the play, assisted Mr. Vale.

At the end of this long day full of contacts with Bumba-meu-Boi participants, I could not fail to note the enthusiasm with which they tried to convey their knowledge of the *brincadeira*: the tenderness with which they touched their costumes, the ox's hide and frame, the admiration in their voices as they spoke about *São João dos Carneirinhos* (Saint John of the Little Lambs), the patron saint of the Bumba-meu-Boi and his miracles. These phenomena were at times emotionally difficult for participants to express verbally. To participants they constitute a body of "unspeakable" which transcend the dramatic and social levels of the merrymaking and touch the spiritual belief cherished by the individual about this cultural manifestation.

My fieldwork was beset with misfortunes that required ingenuity and perseverance to overcome: A toy microphone had to be substituted for a forgotten one. A large supply of new batteries was the wrong size and had to be replaced by used ones of the correct size. One thing I could not overcome was the loss of my slides, which were apparently exchanged, with those of a dentist by the film processing company in Olinda, Pernambuco. I hope he had more use for my slides than I had for his.

Nevertheless, the information I was able to collect on this occasion only nurtured my curiosity and led me to delve further into the subject of Bumba-meu-Boi. My quest for information became an enjoyable activity. I visited local public and private archives and libraries to read all I could find. I held frequent discussions on the subject with my colleagues and students at the university and with Bumba-meu-Boi participants in the community, Department of Tourism and private citizens. With this background, many questions came to mind, questions for which I did not have immediate answers.

Perhaps the most significant data gathering field trip for this project took place after the bulk of the present work had been written. In 1986, the Earthwatch Foundation awarded me a field research grant, and in the summer of the same year, I was joined by a team of twenty-seven volunteers to assist in data gathering and filming of the actual presentation of the Bumba-meu-Boi in Maranhão. With the help of the volunteers, professionals in their own right, I was able to conduct a systematic data gathering on Bumba-meu-Boi in the state of Maranhão more thoroughly than I had done before. During the four-week stay in Maranhão, our agenda was filled with interview meetings with scholars, Bumba-meu-Boi participants, state authorities, and citizens at the market place. We attended presentations of the drama in São Luis and Pindaré; photographed and measured musical instruments, costumes, and related props; documented the preparation process that takes place before the presentation and filmed all the festivities (Saint Peter's parade in the bay and through the city, the greeting of Saint Peter by Bumba-meu-Boi troupes throughout the night as they come to the Saint's chapel by the sea to pay their respect with songs and dances; the square dancing in town squares depicting the palace life of the colony, etc.) which take place during the fifteen day period of the cycle of the *Festas Juninas* (Feasts of the Month of June). We visited state, private, and institutional repositories of Bumba-meu-Boi materials and relics to photograph and photocopy their holdings.

This systematic data gathering was completed with the filming of the entire presentation cycle of the drama, beginning with the "Birth of the Ox" on June 23, and closing with the "Death of the Ox" on July 6, the latter performed early for our benefit. Our audiovisual documentation included 15 hours of reel-to-reel recording of Bumba-meu-Boi songs, and a total of 12 hours of video filming of the actual presentation of the drama in São Luis and in Pindaré. The collected material is representative of the various styles of Bumba-meu-Boi in Maranhão. These are: the *Matraca* style, the *Zabumba* style, the *Orquestra* style, and the newly created theatrical pastiche, the *Boi Barrica*.

Chronological examination of information about Bumba-meu-Boi appearing irregularly in local chronicles since 1850 brings to mind an imaginary curve that graphically represents the process of acceptability of the Bumba-meu-Boi by the ruling class. On a scale from zero to ten, this curve would start at point four in 1850, descend with an intensity of antagonism to point zero by 1861, when Bumba-meu-Boi was banned in the state of Maranhão, maintain this level for six years, and begin its ascent with the tolerance of the state in 1868 to reach the level of total acceptability at point ten by 1965.

In the course of my fieldwork, it became clear to me that students of Brazilian culture have been dealing with Bumba-meu-Boi in a manner similar to that applied to quests for explanations of most Brazilian cultural activities. Bumba-meu-Boi was defined without a thorough investigation of the hidden meaning of its constituent elements and without due consideration given to its intended objectives. It also became evident to me that social meanings, religious associations, origins and historical reconstruction, as well as musical considerations were perfunctorily dealt with and often omitted in studies devoted to Bumba-meu-Boi. I was convinced that there was a need for a comprehensive study that would analyze this folk drama and entertain questions to correct misinformation fostered in the existing literature and to put forth an adequate account of the identity of Bumba-meu-Boi as a cultural manifestation created to fulfill specific Brazilian social functions. Thus, the present project focuses on a socio-historical analysis of the Bumba-meu-Boi, providing its definition, confirming its Brazilian authenticity, revealing its stylistic distinctions, and discussing the process of its assimilation in the state of Maranhão—from its prohibition to its rise in status to the most representative cultural expression of the state.

Scholars cite several advantages to studying the cultural activity of a single group for a given length of time. By concentrating on the *Boi de Zé Vale* troupe in Pindaré, I gained insight into the linguistic community of its people (mostly vaqueiros and fishermen). In turn, this knowledge allowed me to decipher their linguistic transformations and their use of metaphor, to capture the essence of their life experience, and to recognize and interpret signs of social order as they were expressed in the lyrics. Musically, I was able to pinpoint the process of stylistic definition by observing the consistency in the troupe's rendition of the Bumba-meu-Boi. However, this does not imply that acquired knowledge about other Bumba-meu-Boi troupes is obsolete. To the contrary, they strengthened the definition and historical reconstruction of the folk drama; they shed light on stylistic distinction, and revealed the embedded social value of the drama.

As I became more involved with this study, I could not help but observe Bumba-meu-Boi from different theoretical perspectives derived from the humanities. By the time I reached a tangible conclusion, I realized that I had not used a single definitive methodology. A mixture of theoretical premises guided my scrutiny from the fields of anthropology, ethnomusicology, history, sociology, and socio-linguistics to illuminate and sustain my assertions.

Similarities between cultural and social institutions of different societies constituted the core of concern for the nineteenth century diffusionists in the field of ethnology. The diffusionists believed that no society could develop divorced from outside influences.[1] For them, similarities of cultural practices proved that there had been contacts between societies, which allowed for the exchange of cultural elements. Although modern anthropologists have proven this theory to be misleading, its implied objective—quest for the origin of institutions, cultural practices—still underlies modern studies of societies by students of cultures. This is particularly true for societies composed of elements from diverse cultural and racial backgrounds, as is the case in Brazil. The bulk of published material on Brazilian culture focuses on identifying and defining cultural practices, their origins, and the process of their modification in the emerging society.

For decades, the quest for the origin of cultural practices had become a major obsession among students of Brazilian culture, who concentrated most of their effort on this issue to the point of ignoring other pertinent aspects of cultural analysis. Often those obsessed by the search for the origin of cultural elements are led into error and tend to confuse the principles of creation with those of innovation.[2] To believe that all existing cultural practices in a society such as Brazil originated from other societies with which contacts were made or from which members came fosters an archaic theory of extreme diffusionist thought that says all cultural practices originate from one group in one area of the world, and their dissemination is due to contacts made possible by the rise of navigation.[3] To believe the contrary, diffusionists would argue, is to perpetuate the isolation of societies.

There is, however, such a thin semantic line between the sociological concepts of creation and innovation that makes it is difficult to distinguish where they differ from one another. To create implies to originate or to invent new structures constructed mostly with new elements. While the use of old elements is not excluded, they should not bring to mind traces of the structure of which they were integral parts. By definition, to innovate insinuates to modify or to transform an existing structure. Let us examine some examples in order to understand these semantic boundaries and clarify the basis for differentiation between creation and innovation. In Brazil, *Umbanda* is a religious innovation in which African religious practice and belief, Catholicism, and indigenous spiritism constitute the pillars on which the ideological concept of the religion rests. Another relevant example of innovation in Brazilian culture can be encountered in the *samba*, with clear African roots evident in its rhythm and dance variants.[4] The *capoeira*, on the other hand, whose origin continues to challenge scholars, is a creation.

In light of the above discussion, and as will be made evident in the course of the present work, Bumba-meu-Boi falls within the rubric of creation as defined above. The basic legend on which the drama is structured reflects the interaction between masters and slaves in colonial Brazil and does not represent a revived or restructured expression from elsewhere, regardless of the presence of the ox that brings to mind countless other cultural practices in which the ox is used as a unifying element. If the presence of the ox motif is the primary argument used to sustain the theory of Portuguese derivation of the Bumba-meu-Boi advanced by Luis da Câmara Cascudo, then it would not be far-fetched to see Bumba-meu-Boi as also having roots in France or Spain, for instance, where the involvement of the ox in cultural manifestations, both sacred and secular, dates to well before the founding of Brazil.[5]

It is not the symbolic death and resurrection of the ox which constitute the essence of the Bumba-meu-Boi; rather, it is the function for which it was conceived—*to be the slaves' medium of retaliatory expression.* As such, those for whom this purpose was to be served could only have created Bumba-meu-Boi in Brazil. In the course of time, the basic structure of the drama was expanded and modified to meet new social needs, which included, but were not limited to, criticism of the ruling class. Although it is believed to have stemmed from processional manifestations reminiscent of those practiced in Portugal, Bumba-meu-Boi reflects a unique character and structure, different from its alleged prototypes. It is both a social and psychological manifestation, whose uniqueness is reflected in the dual nature of its objectives.

While Bumba-meu-Boi allows its participants to exteriorize aggressions through the hilarious display of social sanctions, it also provides them with an opportunity to express profound devotion to Saint John, Saint Peter, and Saint Mark. The presentation of the Bumba-meu-Boi is an occasion for communal merrymaking and a period of devotion when participants come together, believing in miracles, to seek good fortune from their patron saints. Bumba-meu-Boi is a collective event, which brings members of the community closer to each other. It is also a personal affair in which individuals participate to keep private promises made to the saints and to renew their covenants. Bumba-meu-Boi is also both profane and sacred. This aspect is evident in the role played by the unifying element of the drama—the ox. The latter is the source of deep-seated satire against the ruling class, and the object of devotion that is adorned, sanctified through baptism, and presented to Saint John to serve as a link of covenant between the saints and the participants. Further examination of the Bumba-meu-Boi reveals other values embedded in the characters of this amusement.

From a psychological perspective, the use of the ox in the story line generates the drama and attenuates the impact of the satire on the ruling class. This phenomenon is coupled with the fact that insults are more easily tolerated when sung than when spoken.[6] Subtle satire is incorporated into the roles of the characters representing social authorities and into the manner in which those address these authorities in the play considered to comprise the lowest order in the social hierarchy. Ridiculed characters vary from one region to another, but the most prominent are the Priest, the *Amo* (Master), and the *Cavalo Marinho* (Captain), who represents social authorities in colonial Brazil.

It is interesting to note that having the priest ridiculed in Bumba-meu-Boi in the company of slave owners and police authority confirms the fact that the priests in colonial Brazil owned slaves to work on the plantations. In fact, the Jesuit order was notorious for this practice. This and his hostility against Bumba-meu-Boi motivated Padre Lopes Gama's resentment of the satire of the "servant of God," comical but subtle attack.[7] Obviously, these attacks were directed at the priest's behavior and not at the religion, he represented. Nevertheless, one is still left with a puzzling question concerning the religious connotation, which underlies Bumba-meu-Boi.

The religious implication in Bumba-meu-Boi is easily explained in the states of Bahia and Pernambuco where Bumba-meu-Boi was first performed as a part of the *Reisado*, a series of dramatic sketches presented during the Christmas period in celebration of Epiphany. Although some scholars view this affiliation of the Bumba-meu-Boi with the *Reisado* as corroborating the assumption that this merrymaking is derived from Gil Vicente's *Monólogo do Vaqueiro* (The Cowboy's Monologue), it was never meant to be a Christmas pageant. In fact, nothing in the Bumba-meu-Boi, including the animals (ox and donkey), has a direct association with the nativity. Therefore, the explanation for the detachment of the Bumba-meu-

Boi from the *Reisado* sketches to become associated with Saint John, Saint Peter, and Saint Mark in the states of Maranhão, Pará, and Piauí, can only be found in regional activity such as agriculture, which has a certain impact on the celebration calendar of the Bumba-meu-Boi in these states.

In these states, which belong to the Amazon zone of Brazil, the agricultural cycle ends in June. This is the harvest period for the communities in these areas, which they celebrate in Sunday clothes with music and dance, and the serving of *canjica,* a traditional dish of crushed green corn mixed with cinnamon, milk and sugar and served around a campfire. The consumption of *canjica* is in celebration of the harvest, but the bond fire is reminiscent of the shepherds with whom Saint John is associated.

Several questions about aspects of the Bumba-meu-Boi continue to be ignored by students of Brazilian culture. One of these is why Bumba-meu-Boi is celebrated in conjunction with the observance of Saint John's Day on June 24, Saint Peter's Day on June 29, and Saint Mark's Day on June 30, when it is known, for example, that Saint Mark's Day is celebrated in April? According to one of the answers collected in Pindaré Mirim, the celebration of Bumba-meu-Boi is primarily in conjunction with Saint John, but the two other saints are associated because they are Saint John's friends who were invited to celebrate with an ox on Saint John's birthday.[8] In spite of the importance of this question for the understanding of the religious connotation in Bumba-meu-Boi, there have been no attempts to answer it. However, one thing is certain. This association and the implied devotional observance are both recent practices added to the performance of the Bumba-meu-Boi by participants since the turn of the century, a form of reinterpretation, providing it with a new set of functions and meaning, perhaps to secure its continuity.

Another one of these unanswered questions about Bumba-meu-Boi is related to the decorative motif on the ox's hide. Regardless of the theme depicted on the ox's hide, there is always a star on the forehead of the animal. The meaning of this star is a question often avoided by scholars and even by those who design and reproduce the annual themes on the *lombo do boi* (ox's hide). I recall that while conducting my fieldwork in Maranhão, I raised this question with several owners and participants of Bumba-meu-Boi troupes. However, my curiosity remained unsatisfied. To most of them, there is no specific reason. To those who believe the ox to be an element of devotion between the participant and the saints, the star is a symbol of clarity, purity and sanctity. Still, learned nonprofessionals think of the star as evidence of the Bumba-meu-Boi's distant past association with the *Reisado* sketches. To them, the star on the ox's forehead is reminiscent of the star of Bethlehem, which guided the Magi to the manger.

Although there may be some truth in these observations, I believe there is a simple explanation for this in the story line itself. In the latter, the center of attention is the Master's favorite ox, referred to in the story line as *Boi Estrela*. The practice of placing a star on the ox's forehead could be a visual representation of the ox's name, as with the other thematic material, with an embroidered reproduction on the animal's hide.

Finally yet importantly, what is the reason for the selection of the pregnant woman to be the instigator of the social tension with her impractical request, on the one hand, and her husband's compliance with it, on the other? Addressing this issue has been purposely omitted as being beyond the scope of this study.

INTRODUCTION TO THE SECOND EDITION

The interpretation of the hidden meaning of any Afro-Brazilian cultural manifestations, in general and that of Bumba-meu-Boi in particular, should begin with the understanding of the cultural background of its creators, before delving into any of other aspects. In the "Apresentação" of the third edition of *As Culturas Negras no Novo Mundo* by Arthur Ramos, the editors stressed, "Today, black people are seen in the specificity of their culture, which varies greatly, depending on the area of their origin."[1] Without a doubt, the editors recognized culture as an integral part of Ramos's analysis. The present analysis of Bumba-meu-Boi takes a similar approach to culture, since in any analysis that fails to consider culture in Brazilian cultural manifestations, or in other Latin American societies with a multicultural population, will lead to seriously flawed conclusions.

As I worked on the Portuguese edition of this book, I acquainted myself with the new literature on Bumba-meu-Boi. At the same time, I was drawn to the data (i.e. notes, audio recordings, video, and still photographs) that I recorded during my fieldwork in Brazil more than a decade ago. I found these materials to be of great value, in that they continue to corroborate my initial convictions about the authorship, the origin, and the *raison d'être* of the Bumba-meu-Boi. They shed light on certain questions about the significance of cultural context in the interpretation of this folk drama, and the function/role of Bumba-meu-Boi that were not fully addressed in this book's first edition. In addition, these field notes provide a broader view of the processes of continuity and change that have occurred in the presentation, music, musical instruments, props, and behavior/function associated with Bumba-meu-Boi in the past thirty years. These and other concerns of this folk drama are expanded upon in the appropriate chapters of this new edition.

The Significance of Cultural Context

Attempts on this aspect of Bumba-meu-Boi abound in the existing literature by students from various fields of the Humanities. In this body of literature, two studies, in particular, have attracted my attention, for reasons discussed above. First, writers of these documents have attempted to explain the significance of Bumba-meu-Boi in light of European theoretical paradigms. Secondly, the same writers have failed to give due consideration to the historical aspect, which includes the impact of all phenomena, social and economic, on the carriers of the cultural material, who conceive their cultural manifestation as integral parts of a total expression.[2] In short, their analysis, are carried out, outside of the cultural context.

In his article on "Mãe Catirina's Desire: Psychoanalytic Reflections on the Legend of Bumba-meu-Boi, Brazil," Gerhard Kubik asserts that Bumba-meu-Boi and other cultural manifestations in Brazil, "owe their creative instigation to a specific socio-psychological situation during the time of slavery. That situation varied regionally, and its consequences for the members of different "*nações*" (nations) must have been different."[3] In the same document, Gerhard Kubik endorses the argument about the African slave authorship of Bumba-meu-Boi, Kubik in these words:

> *Those who created Bumba-meu-Boi in Brazil were probably people perpetuating culture traits from central Africa, from Angola in particular, most likely from places with a cattle culture rather than the equatorial forest. I can exclude the possibility that Yoruba or Ewe would have created Bumba-meu-Boi, although—as time passed and transculturation continued—people with a variety of genealogical lines were absorbed and may have played active roles in the drama.*[4]

Addressing the issue of the symbolism in this folk drama, Kubik continues,

> *The core idea [of the folk drama] is that a slave woman's secret desire is to be married by her Master [...] Mãe Catirina needs sex, but sex provided by her 'legitimate' husband is only a poor substitute for her. Her pregnancy could only result in the birth of another slave [...] A slave woman will often have a low opinion of her slave husband and, in many cases, her secret dream will be that the master, un this case the 'white' rancher in power, gets interested in her [...] Put simply, Mãe Catirina needs the 'tongue' as a symbol of the master's sexual power to provide her with a* magic tool, *even literally a medicine to enable her to give birth to a 'good' (probably a light-skinned) child. This is why the theme of pregnancy comes up in the legend.*[5]

Focusing on the theme of the pregnant wife's desire to eat the tongue of the master's favorite animal, Kubik concludes that this request "portrays the common psychodynamic situation in which early 19th century African women in Brazil, reduced to a life in slavery, found themselves."[6] In a paper presented at the American Folklore Society Annual Meeting in Milwaukee (2006), the anthropologist Jelani K. Mahiri avoided to speculate on the authorship of this drama and its social function, and chose to apply the morphological theory proposed by Vlademir Propp in his study of Russian folk tales (2006). He focused his attention on unraveling the structural mechanism of the folk drama and its various versions in the State of Maranhão. To Mahiri, "the utility of a morphological analysis for providing a firmer foundation for such interpretations and to distinguishing more clearly between the narrative content and what may be incorporated during performances of the plot."[7]

There is some validity in both of these paradigms. But, they both have ignored Ramos' warning and failed to examine this merrymaking within its total cultural frame of reference that includes, but is not limited to, socio-economic significance, and its *raison d'être* to the practitioners in time and space. It is then safe to assert that the analysis of the hidden meaning of the Bumba-meu-Boi should be approached from an angle that stresses the meaning of the cultural background of those who created this drama. To date, these aspects of this drama continue to present insurmountable hurtles, for those scholars who prefer to study it according to new theories or in light of those theories that omit to consider the impact of the surviving Africanisms in America in general and in Brazil in particular.

Function/Role of Bumba-meu-Boi

I submit that as it was practiced in 1986 by the "*Rei da Uniao*" troupe in Pindare Mirim, and reproduced herein, the Bumba-meu-Boi plot reflects social interactions, as they existed between classes in colonial Brazil. Socially, the drama was intended to be a mockery of members of the oppressed class of the society against their oppressors. In short, it was intended to ridicule the authority (whites) by the African slaves and the native Indians who were considered nonhuman. Queiroz expands on the function of this merrymaking from a sociological perspective, as she writes,

> *The dominant purpose of the review exercised by the Bumba-meu-Boi is to improve what is deemed bad; It is necessary to make everyday behaviors to approach as much as possible of the ideal models, and the Bumba-meu-Boi is used as a stimulus in this direction.*[8]

In colonial Brazil, there was already a need for social control, a major social concern that involved slaves and their masters. In short, this social interaction between classes needed to be denounced in order to maintain the society alive. In this type of traditional Brazilian society, suggests Queiroz, Bumba-meu-Boi played the role of internal reformer.[9]

Whereas social sanctions were maintained, other insertions into the presentation, such as religious practices (baptism of the ox), were judged pertinent, as its primary *raison d'être* (slavery), became obsolete, after the Brazilian's abolition of slave trade in 1888. With the down play of slavery, the welfare of the community, such as Pindare Mirim, became the central focus of the drama, as Borba Filho put it, "in each region, a local referential text is added [. . .] Bumba-meu-Boi defends the traditional values of group."[10] The concern for local harmony occupied the center stage of topics to be improvised in *toadas*. Writing on the shift in focus of themes in Bumba-meu-Boi, de Queroz writes,

> *The central structure is maintained more or less similar, but each time the little drama and represented, secondary scenes are deleted, others are created, according to the will of the show organizer, or as the important events that have passed and what you want comment [...] the secondary scenes that has been grafted on the main theme are made often for critical uses and customs.*[11]

This insertion by Queiroz is corroborated during the presentation of the drama by the lyrics in the improvised *toadas* that make direct reference to names of the guilty individuals in the community and their offenses. Queiroz asserts, "The function of the Bumba-meu-Boi is then to identify to the population the guilty individuals, all who do not follow the traditional models, and do not perform their duty."[12]

Authorship for Bumba-meu-Boi

I have not shifted my belief about who could have created the Bumba-meu-Boi. Considering the social significance of the eighteenth century period when Bumba-meu-Boi was conceived, those for whom the social function/objective of the play, as discussed above, had to serve could only have been its creators. Seen from this prism, the only logical group that benefited from the objectives of this drama is the African slave, assisted by their Indian counterpart during the colonial Brazil, and not brought from outside. The chain of event in the play sustains this assertion: 1) the slave creates the tension; b) this tension is resolved by the Indian, another oppressed member of the society. Borba Filho recognizes the Brazilian origin of Bumba-meu-Boi, in these words: "Although some European influences are noted in it, its structure, subjects, their types and music are essentially Brazilian."[13] In other words, the plot, subject matter of this folk drama could not have come from elsewhere, and by extension, the above statement also sustains my argument that the African slave created Bumba-meu-Boi.

Going from this premise, then, and in order to understand the hidden meaning in the Bumba-meu-Boi, there is a prerequisite knowledge that one needs to master. In addition, this knowledge is contained within the "African frame of reference" or the "'reference system' of values in terms of which [the drama] is made, performed and interpreted."[14] This African concept of organization is encapsulated in the African oral tradition and passed down from generation to another. Amadou Hampâté Bâ recognizes the impact and the role of the oral tradition in human life in Africa in these terms: "It [oral tradition] is at once religion, knowledge, natural science, apprenticeship in a craft, history, entertainment, recreation, since any point of detail can always take us all the way back to primordial unity."[15] "Oral tradition," concludes Hampâté Bâ, "serves to create a particular type of man, to sculpt the African soul."[16]

As indicated above, in addition to stressing the continuity of the African totemic presence in Bumba-meu-Boi, Arthur Ramos also recognizes the value of cultural context in studying any Afro-Brazilian manifestations. It is in this light that the meaning of Bumba-meu-Boi is herein opined. Surely, the testing of new paradigms in any scientific endeavor cannot be oversimplified, dismissed, or ignored. However, its application should not be recommended to the sacrifice of the cultural context for the sake of new theories. In the words of the editors to Arthur Ramos *As Culturas Negras no Novo Mundo,* "The study is not meant to exalt or blame, but to understand the correct meaning of rich cultures in their origins and that have received other influences in the New World, with acceptances and rejections, in true acculturation process."[17]

This sentiment permeates throughout the present study devoted to the quest for the meaning of Bumba-meu-Boi as a form of an abbreviated communication laden with communal significance. As such, Bumba-meu-Boi has to be approached in this cultural light as a traditional teaching tool, rooted in what is known among the Luba people of the Democratic Republic of Congo, as *"malu a kala"*—past events and/or circumstances. These historical events have occurred, within the ethnic group, and are now serving as the template for the genre of communication called *nsumwinu* (sg. -*lusumwinu*).[18] The elders make frequent use of *nsumwinu* to convey—*lunganyi*—a cultural wisdom/knowledge, to members of the younger generation.

Therefore, to decipher the intended knowledge contained in the *nsumwinu*, it is necessary, *a priori*, to be familiar with the ethnic history, and to be well versed in cultural knowledge of the ethnic group. This prerequisite knowledge is mandatory, because *nsumwinu* are formulated on the ground of past occurrences in the ethnic group. Seen from this perspective, challenges presented by Bumba-meu-Boi or any other cultural manifestations created/innovated by Afro-Brazilians require, as suggested by Ramos, to be familiar with the area of the original culture of those who have created it, while taking into consideration any modification that may have occurred to that culture in the New World as a result of transculturation. In short, the hidden meaning, i.e., the moral of the story, the lesson to be retained from the Bumba-meu-Boi drama can only be properly understood within the African frame of reference.

NOTES

1. See Gomes, Laura G., Livia Barbosa and José Augusto Drummond, eds. *O Brasil não é para Principiantes* (2000).

2. John Beattie. *Other Cultures: Aims, Methods and Achievements in Social Anthropology.* New York: Free Press of Glencoe, 1964, pp. 8-11; Robert H. Lowie. *The History of Ethnological theory.* New York: Holt, Rinehart and Winston, 1937, pp. 156-195.

3. Kazadi wa Mukuna & Tiago de Oliveira Pinto. "The Study of African Musical Contribution to Latin America and the Caribbean: A Methodological Guideline." A paper developed in collaboration with the "Grupo de Trabajo – CIDEM." *The World of Music* 32, 3 (1990), pp. 103-104.

4. Discussed in Grafton Elliot Smith. *In the Beginning: The Origin of Civilization.* New York: William Morrow and Company, 1928, pp. 31-46. See also Leo Frobenius. "The Origin of African Civilization," in *Smithsonian Institution Annual Report,*1898.

5. Kazadi wa Mukuna. *Contribuição Bantu na Música Popular Brasileira: Perspectivas Etnomusicológicas.* São Paulo: Terceira Marem 2000, p. 19.

6. Sir James George Frazer. *The Golden Bough: A Study in Magic and Religion,* 2nd Ediction. London: The McMillan, 1900.

7. Alan P. Merriam. The Anthropology of Music. 7th edition. Illinois: Northwestern University Press, 1978, pp. 190-193.

8. Padre Lopes Gama. "A Estulotice do Bumba-meu-Boi." O Carapuceiro no. 2, 11 de janeiro de 1840.

9. See field notes, Pindaré Mirim July 6, 1986.

10. Editors. "Apresentação," in Arthur Ramos. As Culturas Negras no Novo Mundo. São Paulo: Companhia Editorial Nacional, 3rd ed., 1979, p. xii.

11. Kazadi wa Mukuna and Tiago de Oliveira Pinto, op. cit., p. 103.

12. Gerhard Kubik. "Mãe Catirina's Desire: Psychoanalytic Reflections on the Legend of Bumba-meu-Boi, Brazil." Psychoanalytic Review , 95 (6), De-

cember 2008, p. 1037.

13. Ibid. p. 1037.
14. Ibid. pp. 1040-1041.
15. Ibid. pp. 1035-1044.
16. Anonymous. "Of Ox, Slaves, Cowboys and Indians: Plot, Performance and Power in the Bumba-meu-Boi of Brazil." Unpublished manuscript.
17. Maria Isaura Pereira de Queiroz. "O bumba-meu-Boi, Manifestacao de Teatro Popular no Brasil." *O Campesinato Brasileiro*. Petropolis: Editora Vozes, p. 168.
18. Idem.
19. Hermilo Borba Filho. Apresentação do Bumba-meu-Boi . Recife: Imprensa Universitaria, 1967, p. 11.
20. Maria Isaura P. Queiroz. "O Bumba-meu-Boi, Manifestação de Teatro Popular no Brasil," in *o Campesinato Brasileiro* . Petrópolis: Editora Vozes, 1973, p. 160.
21. Ibid., p. 168.
22. Hermilo Borba Filho. *Apresentação do Bumba-meu-Boi*. Recife: Imprensa Universitária, 1967, p. 9.
23. Portia K. Maultsby. "Africanisms in African=American Music," in Joseph E. Holloway, ed. *Africanisms in American culture*. Bloomington: Indiana University Press, 1990; Kwabena Nketia. "African Roots of Music in the Americas: An African View," in Ethnomusicology and African Music: Collected Papers – Vol. 1 – Modes of Inquiry and Interpretation. Accra (Ghana): Afram Publications, 2005, p. 324.
24. Amadou Hampaté Bâ, "The Living Tradition," in General History of Africa—I: Methodology and African Prehistory edited by Joseph Ki-Zerbo. Los Angeles: University of California Press, 1981, p. 168.
25. Ibid., p. 168.
26. Arthur Ramos. *As Culturas Negras no Novo Mundo*. Rio de Janeiro: Civilização Brasileira, 1937, p. XII.
27. For a more detailed description of nsumwinu , see Kazadi wa Mukuna. "'Nsumwinu': Meaning and Role in the Structural Composition of Melodies in the Urban Music of the Democratic Republic of the Congo." *África: Revista de Centro de Estudos Africanos, Número Especial 2012: África Única e Plural – Melanges em Homenagem ao Professor Fernando Augusto*

Albuquerque Mourão, Organizador Kabengele Munanga - Universidade de São Paulo, Brasil, 2012, pp. 199-210.

CHAPTER I

An Argument for the Brazilian Origin of Bumba-meu-boi

The literal English translation of the Portuguese expression *bumba-meu-boi* is "dance my ox." Bumba-meu-Boi (referred to also as the Boi) is not just a dance, although that is an important part of its full meaning. Comparing it with cultural manifestations from other parts of the world with similar motifs, we see similarities to the French epic poem *Chanson de Roland* set during the during the eighth century reign of Charlemagne, but the message and intended *raisons d'être* of Bumba-meu-Boi are difficult to decipher. When explored from a dramatic perspective, Bumba-meu-Boi also brings to mind a medieval mystery play (pageant) that has lost its element of surprise. As conceived and presented in Brazil, Bumba-meu-Boi is a secular folk drama with music and dance, whose thematic material is built around the symbolic death and resurrection of an ox. It functions as a means of social control, reflecting the social interaction between classes with a focus on the criticism of the upper classes by the lower. For its participants, it also provides a setting for renewing a personal covenant with an adopted saint.

The task of the present chapter is to assert the Brazilian authenticity of Bumba-meu-Boi by defining its birthplace in Brazil, placing its probable author, and describing the pattern of its dissemination throughout the country. The chapter presents a detailed review of the published theories concerning the origin of the Boi in Brazil and its significance in the state of Maranhão, explores the historical depth of its meaning, and discusses the socio-cultural approaches applied in this study. New arguments are supported by empirical data from the field and conclusions derived from personal observations of the Boi.

CHAPTER I

ORIGIN THEORIES

One of the most important issues occupying Brazilian folklore scholars over the past fifteen years concerns the origin of Bumba-meu-Boi. An examination of the existing literature dealing with this topic reveals some conflicting theories. The first of these, advanced by Guilherme Theodore Pereira de Melo, attributes the origin of Bumba-meu-Boi to Portugal and affirms that it is a variation of a sixteenth-century play, *Monólogo do Vaqueiro*, presented by its author, Gil Vicente, on June 8, 1502, on the steps of Dona Maria's castle on the occasion of the birth of Prince Dom João, King Dom Manuel's firstborn (1947, 59). In Brazil this theory is given credence in Bahia and Pernambuco, where Bumba-meu-Boi is associated with Christmas. Discussing the origin of Bumba-meu-Boi, M. I. Pereira de Queiroz affirms that this is part of the *Reisados* celebrated during Epiphany; *Noites dos Reis* (Nights of Kings) is composed of short sketches whose story revolves around the ox. She writes:

> *In Brazil, the ox of processions and of ancient bull races in Portugal had transformed itself into the principal character of a dramatic dance...Thus the parade of the Bumba-meu-Boi would be, perhaps, directly descended from Portuguese processions; on the other hand, the bull dancing during the spectacle...might be reminiscent of the hidden bull fights.*[1]

Luis da Câmara Cascudo also espouses the European origin of Bumba-meu-Boi when he compares it to the Portuguese *tourinha* (imitative bull run or ride). He writes:

> Tourinhas *were the same as* touros de canastra [*basket bulls*], *make believe bulls...disguised with a colored cover, having a man inside, moving it, driving it at young men who dodge to shouts, imitating without danger the true herd of bulls. There it was, then, in Portugal, one of the vivid elements of the Bumba-meu-Boi, idle and playful.*[2]

Similar views are shared by Michel Simon,[3] who also believes that

Bumba-meu-Boi came from the Portuguese *bois de armação*, and by Gastão Bettencourt, who would like us to believe that the early form of Bumba-meu-Boi came from Portugal.[4] Luis Chaves refutes Câmara Cascudo's suggestion and reexamines the definition of the terms *tourinha* and its derivative, showing that Cascudo and Michel Simon are comparing two manifestations of a different nature. Chaves concludes that the *tourinha* not only lacks an *enredo* (theme), but also differs from Bumba-meu-Boi in that the latter contains the sacrifice of the ox.[5]

To entertain the theory that Bumba-meu-Boi did originate in Europe is to raise several questions, among them: (a) Why would Europeans foster a play in the New World in which they are the villains? (b) Why is it that since its introduction in Brazil, Bumba-meu-Boi has always been associated with slaves or the Black population? An 1840 article by Padre Lopes Gama gives his description of the presentation of Bumba-meu-Boi and points out, "*Um negro metido de baixo d'uma baieta é o boi...*" (A Black person hidden inside a shaggy fabric made of wool is the ox...).[6] "This year [there] appeared an amusement by Blacks known as the Boi, prohibited by the police a few years ago for being uncivilized."[7] These and other similar statements encountered in the literature attest that Bumba-meu-Boi could not have been inherited from Portugal. It is difficult to believe that the enslaved African assumed an expression with which he had nothing to identify himself culturally.

The second theory, formulated by Arthur Ramos, dismisses de Melo's suggestion and indicates that Bumba-meu-Boi has three origins: African, Amerindian, and European. Discussing the African origin, Ramos stresses that Bumba-meu-Boi contains totemic elements from there. He states:

> *Recall that psychoanalytically, the totemic animal is the symbol of the Father...But, it is in the Bumba-meu-Boi that the totemic complexes reveal themselves with more evidence...In this manifestation, the death of the ox [Father] is the leitmotif. The children kill the father...The African Black kept these ritual feasts in his subconscious and, through the principle of repetition, expended them periodically in popular manifestations which he encountered*

in the new home.[8]

This same theory, shared by Edison Carneiro, is paraphrased by Ramos in *As Culturas Negras no Novo Mundo*: "I have previously pointed out the mistake of those students who connect [Bumba-meu-Boi] with the ox of the manger, of Iberian origin, and to the half-breed *vaqueiro* cycle. I believe the African has brought a fundamental contribution. The ox totem is widely disseminated among various Bantu peoples [the Geroa ox among the Ba-Nyaneka, for example].[9] The third theory, suggested by Domingos Vieira Filho, recognizes the influence of the three racial groups in Bumba-meu-Boi and asserts: "Origins of the bumba are confusedly lost in time. What can be advanced with certainty is that the merrymaking was born in [Brazil], as a logical consequence of colonial formation, with the influence of the three races which forged the nationality."[10] The enslaved African, concludes Vieira Filho, made the choice of the ox as the central theme of Bumba-meu-Boi, because both had experienced a similar fate in colonial Brazil. In Vieira Filho's terms, "the Negro slave was the bull's brother in suffering and in work.[11] I concur partially with this theory but not for the reasons advanced by its author. My own reasons are discussed below.

The quest for the origin of Bumba-meu-Boi continues to be the topic of vivid discussion among scholars throughout Brazil, but it takes a different dimension in Maranhão, where the folk drama is celebrated annually. Three of the most prominent scholars in São Luis, who have been working on the subject from various perspectives, met in a roundtable debate on July 7, 1986: Mr. José Valdelino Cécio from the Fundação Cultural do Maranhão; Professor Américo Azevedo Neto, a journalist, author, and member of the Academy of Letters of Maranhão; and Professor Jomar Moraes, author and president of the Academy of Letters and secretary of culture of the state. Américo states:

> *The fact of a bull that dances in the center of a circle of people who are drinking, singing and dancing is not peculiar to Maranhão or Brazil. It exists in various countries in the world. In Portugal, there is a popular merrymaking with an ox, which resembles Bum-*

> ba-meu-Boi in Maranhão in its gathering process, which would be the guarnecer; in its opening procession of characters, which would be the lá vai; in its acknowledgement of the place of presentation, which would be the eu cheguei. I believe that the history of the Bumba-meu-Boi in Brazil is related to the Jesuit's cycle of catechism.[12]

Dismissing this conjecture, Jomar Moraes asserts: "Taking the structuralist point of view, I think that these external aspects of the *Boi Apts*, of the *tourinha*, and other European celebrations of the ox are not sufficient to determine that our Bumba-meu-Boi comes from them. I believe that our Boi has a popular origin. It is of the people" (Jomar Moraes recorded at the roundtable debate, São Luis, July 7, 1986). Stressing the difference between the learned and the popular approaches, Américo rebuts:

> It is evident that Bumba-meu-Boi has a learned origin. This origin is implanted in the catechism cycle of the Jesuits who took advantage of the amusement, which was also educational. It contains a moral lesson while at the same time it has all the characteristics of a theatrical piece.[13]

There are certain elements of validity in each of these hypotheses, but all ignore the essence of why Bumba-meu-Boi was created. Perhaps the best position among these arguments is Cécio Valdelino's. He sums up the discussion with a more neutral position: "The problem of the origin of the Bumba-meu-Boi is not important. In the midst of this confusion with a myriad of hypotheses, none of which is truly confirmed, forces us to believe in a little bit from one and the other."[14]

Fundamentally, it is important to understand that the presence of an ox in human mythology is universal. It is mentioned in the literature and legends of societies ranging from prehistoric and preliterate to the most modern and highly technological. Regardless of the tradition in which it is encountered, the ox generally stands for industry, patience, and strength, and is often the principal medium of trade as well as symbol of wealth.[15]

CHAPTER I

THE OX IN BRAZIL

Since its introduction into Brazil in 1530 and its eventual dissemination throughout the country, the ox has been a prominent factor in economic development and territorial expansion. Since 1530, cattle were exploited in every possible way in Brazil's economic and social development. The ox was an integral element of the sugarcane mills that made Brazil the foremost sugar producer of the world, a position that the country enjoyed for more than half a century. It was the sole source of fertilizer for the tobacco plantations, whose crops also dominated the international market, and it was important in the triangular slave trade from 1600 until 1701. Domestically, it served as a source of transportation, plantation work, and food; and its hide was the source of clothing, bedding, and ropes.[16] In fact, the commercialization of ox hide was equaled only in the twentieth century by Brazilian gold and coffee.

The geographical location of the cattle industry shifted to accommodate its primary market. During the sugarcane period (1530–1650) and the tobacco period (1600–1750), the industry thrived in the São Francisco River Valley in Bahia and Pernambuco, as well as in the Capitania of São Vicente and other coastal areas where sugar mills were established. During the leather commerce period (1720–1890), cattle raising was concentrated in the north and northeast hinterlands—notably Ceará, Piauí, and Maranhão by the end of the seventeenth and the beginning of the eighteenth centuries—and in the southern Rio Grande do Sul region from the beginning of the eighteenth century.

For a century and a half, until 1850, Bahia was the sugar capital of Brazil and of the world. One can only guess the number of cattle in this region, especially when a normal sugarcane complex had to have at least twice as many cattle as slaves in order to satisfy the complex's considerable energy demands.[17] By the mid-seventeenth century, cattle raising had reached its apogee in the São Francisco River Valley. Yet the demand for cattle grew in conjunction with the increasing number of sugar mills, new economic developments such as mining and cotton production, and population growth in the rest of the country.

As these centers of economic development shifted, they pulled cattle industry with them. Answering this demand, cattlemen followed two routes in their quest for pastureland. Toward the end of the seventeenth century, one route followed the São Francisco River toward Minas Gerais, reaching the state of Piauí, where favorable conditions made this state the most important cattle region and producer of meat (even supplying the state of Bahia). The progression did not end in Piauí, though. It crossed the Rio Parnaiba and reached Maranhão, where it met with those coming up from the coast along the Itapecuru River. On the second route, cattlemen came into Ceará, mingling with those coming in the opposite direction from Pernambuco, mostly following the coastal bend.[18]

The beginning of the seventeenth century saw a shift in the international economy. Brazilian sugar had always been the prime commodity, but now it was supplanted by Bahian tobacco, offered in exchange for slaves from the "Costa da Mina" in Africa. Verger states:

> *In Bahia, since the seventeenth century, tobacco plants had increased in importance, and attempted to surpass those of sugarcane. The latter flourished more in Pernambuco. The first and second quality tobacco was reserved for exportation to Portugal…That of the third category, considered reject, was left for local consumption and for exchange with Africa. This third class tobacco had practically no market except in the four ports of Costa da Mina.*[19]

This trade with Africa became very important, especially after 1698, when the discovery of gold in the states of Bahia and Minas Gerais required a frequent replenishment of slaves, whose average productive lifespan was only seven years. In Bahia, tobacco was being cultivated in large quantities to satisfy various demands; cattle were the primary source of fertilizer. This is also the period when cattle raising paralleled the tobacco culture in growth, as cattle hides were also used for wrapping bales of tobacco designated for export.[20]

In spite of the paramount role cattle played during the Costa da Mina cycle and in Bahia, the importance and dissemination of cattle raising began to decline. Several factors contributed to a ban on cattle raising on tobacco farms: Besides the fact that cattle had begun to invade plantations and destroy crops, the land could instead be used to cultivate manioc to feed the slaves. The Portuguese Crown settled this dispute in favor of agriculture, effectively pushing cattle raising inland.

> *[On the plantations, there were] no barbed wire, the great pacifying element and protector of cultivation in the field. This is one of the reasons that cattle raising withdrew inland, far from mills, sugarcane and manioc plantations and into poorer lands that could not be used for any kind of cultivation by the increasing number of mills on the coast. A royal letter of 1701 even prohibited the raising of cattle within sixty kilometers of the coast.*[21]

In the aforementioned activities, the cattle participation was secondary, although at times it may have been considered indispensable to the development of these activities. However, other aspects of cattle utilization later appeared in Brazil during the so-called *Civilização do Couro* (Leather Civilization), beginning in the second decade of the eighteenth century. During this period, which lasted well into the twentieth century, the importance of leather products can be seen not only in commerce with foreign countries, but also in domestic consumption of clothing, furniture, rope, and other items. In international commerce, leather was one of eight principal products (along with coffee, sugar, cotton, tobacco, rubber, cacao, and mate [tea]) exported by Brazil for nearly sixty years. From 1821 to 1889, leather exports ranged from 13.6 percent of these eight commodities in the first ten years to 3 percent during the last decade.

In spite of its significant role in Brazil's social life and economic development, no mention is found in published sources or interviews of the elevation of cattle to a valued or supernatural position in the folk culture. References in Arthur Ramos's writing are mere speculation and a misinterpretation of the *Boi Geroa* practice between the Ba-Nyaneka in southern Angola.[22] There is insufficient evidence to attest to the possibility that those enslaved Africans who were involved in the development of Bumba-meu-Boi in the sugar mills were from the same region of southern Angola. Equally invalid is

Mário de Andrade's assertion about Bumba-meu-Boi: "Although it is not native to Brazil, but that of Portugal and Europe, and coincides with the African magical festivities, the dramatic dance of Bumba-meu-Boi has become the most complex, peculiar, and original of all our dramatic dances."[23] José Ribeiro de Souza's characterization of Bumba-meu-Boi can also be dismissed for the same lack of convincing evidence. "Bumba-meu-Boi," writes de Souza, "and its various modalities are totemic dances. They symbolize the death and the resurrection, in a satire of the negro against white oppression, in the manner of *Congos, Caboclinhos, Cheganças,* and *Guerreiros.*"[24]

While these theories of origin may have some validity, I believe that as conceived and celebrated in Brazil, Bumba-meu-Boi reflects an image of interaction between social classes in colonial Brazil. In more precise terms, Bumba-meu-Boi is a retaliatory statement from oppressed members of society to denounce and ridicule their oppressors. It reflects a character and a structure different from those of its alleged prototypes. It is social and secular, psychological and religious, as well as a collective and personal manifestation sustained by the complex nature of its objectives. While Bumba-meu-Boi allows participants to exteriorize aggression through humorous displays of social taboos, today it also provides them with an opportunity to express profound devotion to Saint John, Saint Peter, and Saint Mark. As a collective and social manifestation, a presentation of Bumba-meu-Boi is an occasion for communal merrymaking. The ox was a symbol of power and source of wealth during the Leather Civilization, and acted as the focal point for expressing a deep-seated ridicule of the ruling class. Over time, the ox also became an object of devotion that is adorned, sanctified through baptism, and offered to Saint John to serve as a symbol of covenant between the saints and the participants. It is both a unifying motif and a way of attenuating the impact of mockery.

To understand the essence of this characterization, let us look at a version of the storyline that provides the dramatic base for Bumba-meu-Boi. The three racial groups and two social classes found in colonial Brazilian society are present in it. The ruling class characters include the Portuguese Amo and his wife Dona Maria– owners

CHAPTER I

of the ranch on which the story unfolds—the priest, and the chief of police (or Cavalo Marinho); the lower class characters include Pai Francisco, the daring enslaved African, his wife Mãe Catirina, the Indigenous medicine-man, the *vaqueiros*, and the servants. The social interaction between them is depicted through a chain of events that requires the intervention of each racial character to restore social harmony. This version of the story was recorded during 1980–1981 field trips in the district of Pindaré, located 250 km south of São Luis, the capital of Maranhão, and is common throughout the region.

On a ranch owned by a Portuguese rancher [Amo] and his wife Dona Maria, dwelt the slave Pai Francisco [also called Nêgo Chico], his pregnant wife Mãe Catirina, and other slaves. The Amo has a favorite bull, referred to in the legend as Boi Estrela [favorite bull] or Fama Real [Royal Fame]. One day Mãe Catirina has a craving for an ox's tongue. Making her desire known to her husband, Mãe Catirina specifies that the tongue must be that of the master's favorite animal. Concerned for the health of his unborn child, Pai Francisco leads the master's bull into the woods, where he kills it and takes the tongue to his wife, who cooks and eats it. The next day, the master, realizing that his favorite bull is missing, summons all his vaqueiros *and slaves together to ask if anyone has seen it. One of them informs him that he has seen Pai Francisco taking Boi Estrela into the woods, from whence, minutes later, a gunshot is heard. Searching the woods, they encounter the remains of the bull. Infuriated by the sight of his dead animal, the master orders the director of Indians to arrest Pai Francisco. Before undertaking such a dangerous mission, the director of Indians seeks a blessing from the priest. Addressing Pai Francisco, the master orders him to bring his bull back to life, or die himself. A Portuguese doctor enters the scene and, in vain, attempts to resurrect the bull. Finally an Indian shaman is summoned. He lays his hands on the animal, which arises, and they all dance joyfully through the night.*

N.B.: At the last presentation of the year, the shaman's magic does not work and the bull is destroyed and its meat symbolically dis-

tributed among those present [participants and audience].

An examination of Bumba-meu-Boi from a psycho-sociological standpoint reveals the embedded concept of hierarchy as a reflection of the coexisting ethnic and racial groups within the colonial society, where this social hierarchy is caricatured in the essence of the play. It may be said that the hierarchy is minimized, and its boundaries are obliterated through the play's interaction. Bumba-meu-Boi is also a means of challenging the authority of the ruling class. Closer examination of the core of the play reveals that, having no other recourse to assert their rights, the oppressed members of society created a play in which despised authorities are caricatured and denounced. The objective of the drama, then, is the denunciation of the ill-behaved members of the ruling class and the catharsis of deep-seated resentment towards them through satire.

Starting with Mãe Catirina's unreasonable request and Pai Francisco's daring compliance with it, every scene of the drama depicts ridicule of the authorities in one form or another. The killing of the master's favorite bull is indeed an act to provoke his anger. But the adopted solution to pacify the situation reflects the oppressed class mockery of the white man's medicine. In the play, the Portuguese doctor's attempts to resurrect the bull fail, and it is the indigenous healer's magic that succeeds in bringing the bull back to life. In light of this interpretation, which reveals the hidden drama embedded in the two most significant contrasting episodes—provocation and pacification—of the entire drama, it can be deduced that Bumba-meu-Boi was created to serve as a medium to criticize social injustices as witnessed by its author. Américo explains:

> *In the Cocoa region near Bacabal and Coroatá, the play is interpreted in such a way that when the ox recuperates nobody pays attention to Chico and Catirina. But in this zone of Itapecurú do Mearim, Catirina aborts while the bull recuperates. It appears to me as an attempt at denouncement. Until today, the landlord takes better care of the cattle than of the* vaqueiro. *A cow is ill, so call the veterinarian; but if the* vaqueiro *is not feeling well, he should drink an herb tea to see if he improves. This lack of assistance to*

the vaqueiro *and the exaggerated care of the cattle appears to me to be what is revealed in the plot.*²⁵

Drawing researchers' attention to the scrutiny of Africanisms in the culture of Latin America and the Caribbean, Tiago de Oliveira Pinto and I proposed a methodological guideline that stressed the importance of the conceptual world of the carriers of cultural material as affected by the history of the new (Brazilian) society in these terms:

*The identification of African elements in the musical fabric of Latin America should also take into consideration the historical aspect which includes the impact of all phenomena, social and economic, on the carriers of the cultural material. This sustains the fact that a musical expression is indeed a product of the influence of these phenomena on the conceptual level of its makers. To the latter, music is not conceived as mere organization of sounds, but rather as integral parts of a total expression, which includes languages, dances, movements, games, and special behaviors, pertaining to a dynamic society.*²⁶

Implicit in this methodological concept are three focuses of interpretation, each of which requires a precise analysis of historical, cultural, and conceptual processes of evolution of Africanisms in the Americas. These are: (a) persistence/continuity; (b) innovation/transformation; and (c) creation/concept. In the first category, one seeks physical materials (e.g., musical instruments, rhythmic patterns, dance steps, cultural manifestations, or religious practices) that exist in the New World as extensions of a specific area and culture in Africa. In the second, African musical and cultural expressions have been modified or reinterpreted in the new society. In the latter aspect, physical African elements are absent, but the new expression is structured according to the African concept of organization. Discussing Africanisms in African-American music, Portia Maultsby concludes the following:

A study of African-American music from the seventeenth through the twentieth centuries reveals that African retention in African-

> *American music can be defined as a core of conceptual approaches. Fundamental to these approaches is the axiom that music making is conceived as a communal/participatory group activity. Black people create, interpret, and experience music out of an African frame of reference—one that shapes musical sound, interpretation, and behavior and makes Black music traditions throughout the world a unified whole.*[27]

It is within the framework of these methodological guidelines that the argument about the African authorship of Bumba-meu-Boi is formulated, seeking evidence of the principles of organization that perpetuate Africanisms in the Diaspora. Two facts are certain. First, in spite of Américo's argument that Bumba-meu-Boi could not have been created spontaneously but according to the rules and regulations of the theatre, Bumba-meu-Boi was not an individual but a communal creation.[28] Second, Bumba-meu-Boi cannot have originated among the ruling class, but rather is a creation of the lower class. It is certain the enslaved African, considered less than human and who had to be enslaved in order to "protect" the indigenous person's soul was being saved by the Jesuits, would be more likely than the indigenous to have come up with such an expression because of his contact with the ruling class.

Within the drama itself, one can also find sufficient evidence in support of Bumba-meu-Boi as an enslaved African creation. One element is that the daring slave and his wife have names—Francisco and Catirina—and another is the choice to deliver satire through singing. When addressed to a superior, this form of dramatization is a widespread practice among African cultures. "In song," writes Alan Merriam, "the individual or the group can express deep-seated feelings not permissibly verbalized in other contexts."[29] Similar practices are also commonplace among the Bashi in the Democratic Republic of Congo, the Luo in Kenya, and Zulu in South Africa, to name a few. In the Northeast of the Democratic Republic of Congo, for example, the Mangbetu people use a repertoire of court songs called the *Amangbetu Olya*, sung to the king by his subjects and members of the court, to indicate a problem, make a request, criticize him, or simply ask for alcoholic beverages. Discussing similar practices among the Chopi of Mozambique, Hugh Tracy writes: "You can say publicly in songs what you cannot say privately to a man's face...and so this is one of the ways African society takes to maintain a spiritually healthy community."[30] In Bumba-meu-Boi, members of the ruling class were satirized through this African concept.

Most who are acquainted with the history of what are hailed today as Brazil's national folk expressions will agree that Bumba-meu-Boi has suffered trials similar to the samba and capoeira, known to have been respectively innovated and created by slaves. Along with João Batista Borges Pereira, I discuss the nature of these trials; for instance, in the state of Maranhão alone, a considerable number of notices in local newspapers reveal problems that faced Bumba-meu-Boi before the upper class accepted it as a characteristic folk expression.[31]

DISSEMINATION

When and where Bumba-meu-Boi was first performed remains unknown, although seventeenth and eighteenth century sugarcane plantations and mills of Bahia and Pernambuco continue to be designated as the period and the sites of its first occurrence. José de Jesus Santos identifies this period as the "golden period of the cattle cycle, in Northeast, North and South, when the lives of the inhabitants of these regions were profoundly interrelated to the cattle-raising."[32] In reference to Bumba-meu-Boi in the state of Maranhão, Domingos Vieira Filho includes in his "Folclore do Maranhão" a similar assertion with no commitment to the identification of the time and place.

> *Bumba-meu-Boi...represents a reminder of the pastoral phase in the colony, during which the ox was the important economic agent, driving herds of cattle in the vast pastures of the country's inland, implanting ranches and corrals which were often the initial nucleus of the important settlements.*[33]

On the other hand, in the 1954 edition of his *Diccionario do Folclore Brasileiro*, da Câmara Cascudo avoids dealing directly with the issue and points out that Henry Koster, who lived in a mill, does not mention this merrymaking among those he assisted and recorded during the first decade of the nineteenth century. However, in the 1962 edition of the same dictionary, the author asserts that Bumba-meu-Boi could be dated from the last decades of the eighteenth century and that its milieu was the coast, sugar mills, and cattle ranches, from where it radiated to the interior.[34] So, Henry Koster's omission of any reference to this play in his writings, as referred to by da Câmara Cascudo, raises other questions—as does Padre Lopes Gama's 1840 judgment of the Boi as doltish.[35] Most likely, Koster's omission can be attributed to his ignorance of its existence, due to the fact that when he lived in the mills this play was still in its embryonic stage and was not yet known as Bumba-meu-Boi.

As for Padre Lopes Gama, he formulates the following statement:

Until now such amusement does not rate above a popular merrymaking, extremely tasteless; but until a few years ago no Bumba-meu-Boi was considered good if it did not include a character dressed as a clergyman, and sometimes with rochet and stole to play as dumb in the function.[36]

It is pertinent to point out that the essence of Padre Lopes Gama's article was not to introduce Bumba-meu-Boi to his readers in Pernambuco, but rather to express his unhappiness with the fact that the servant of God was the butt of a joke. Significantly, however, he refers to Bumba-meu-Boi pageant as "well known" in this region. By utilizing the expression, "until a few years ago," to denote when the presence of the new character was first noticed in the Boi, he is implying a time factor that should be taken back at least about ten years. This interpretation seems wise in light of an article by the same author in which he makes similar usage of temporal expression: "It was during the reign of the General Governor José Cesar de Meneses, in Pernambuco, that *zabumba* appeared for the first time."[37] (The *zabumba* is a membranophone to be discussed in conjunction with stylistic distinction of Bumba-meu-Boi in Maranhão.) But the chronology of governors in Pernambuco places de Meneses in the early eighteenth century (1709), and more than a century had already gone by. On these grounds, one could establish the birth date of the Boi by the middle of the latter half of the eighteenth century (ca. 1780). This is the period when the Leather Civilization was at its peak in the São Francisco River Valley (Bahia and Pernambuco), and its repercussions were being felt as far north as Pará, Maranhão, and the interior of Ceará.

The dissemination of Bumba-meu-Boi in Brazil did not occur simultaneously with the expansion of cattle raising, although it did follow the same routes. From the valley of the São Francisco River—the first Brazilian region to receive cattle and the site of the earliest mention of the play—Bumba-meu-Boi followed the cattle into Ceará, Piauí, Maranhão and Pará. Its introduction in these states may not have occurred in the same sequence as the introduction of cattle. In Maranhão, for example, Cyro Falcão dates the first rehearsal of the Boi from the period of the 1838–1841 uprising in the interior of the state, known as the Balaiada Rebellion. From his research, Domingos Vieira Filho concludes that in Maranhão, Bumba-meu-Boi probably dates from the latter years of the eighteenth century as a form of merrymaking for slaves on ranches and in sugar mills.[38] In 1858 the Maranhão newspaper *O Globo* had already published an article describing Bumba-meu-Boi as indecent, barbarous, grotesque and worthy of being banned. In the state of Pará, *A Voz Paraense* refers to the slaves' play of the time, called *Boi Caiado*; in Santa Catarina, José Boiteux accounts for another version of the Boi known as *Boi-de-Mamão* in 1871.[39] Other names such as *Boi-Bumbá, Boi de Reis, O Boi, Boi-Calemba*,[40] *Boi Misterioso*,[41] *Boi Pintadinho*, and *Boi Moleque*,[42] chronicled in diverse sources, attest to the presence of the amusement in other states of the nation.

EARLY FORMS

The original form of Bumba-meu-Boi, as first performed in the eighteenth century sugarcane complexes, has attracted very little scholarly attention due to the lack of substantial supportive data, either written or oral. Based on the large amount of descriptive literature on Bumba-meu-Boi, one would expect to encounter more than a handful of authors who have devoted passages in their writings to speculating about the early form of the Boi. The oldest written document on the Boi does not provide a full description of the amusement in its earliest form, but rather only sketches an idea of the nineteenth-century version, which included a comic character representing the priest. In lieu of delving into Padre Lopes Gama's 1840 version of the Boi, let us now turn our attention to analyses of versions recorded by contemporary scholars.

Discarding the assumption that the Boi was derived from Gil Vicente's *Monólogo do Vaqueiro*, in which he states that Vicente had copied from the dances of *Festas do Aguinaldo* (Festivities of the Birth of an Ox), de Melo classifies Bumba-meu-Boi among the *Reisados*, and concludes that *Reisado* is the origin of the early dance of Bumba-meu-Boi.[43] In the same document, Pereira de Melo gives an account of what he calls *Rancho do Boi*, which he hosted in 1906 at his home in São Tomé de Paripe. It is pertinent to reproduce the chronology of this *Rancho do Boi* to demonstrate that what do scholars often refer to as Bumba-meu-Boi in Brazil is a substantially different amusement with a different intent:

I closed the doors, as is customarily done, in order to let the initial song begin, which ended with their outburst of the indecent

Open the door

And the window also

That I want to enjoy

The color of the shinbone

Lady of the house

It's best for you to give

Bottles of wine

Sweet of araça [*a wild fruit*]

I had to open them again to start the performance. While they were singing these obscenities, everyone came in, characters and choral singers, leaving only the ox and the vaqueiro *outside. They followed the set of four allegories successively sung in solo by diverse figures of the* rancho. *At the end, the shrill sound of a whistle establishes the needed silence, and calls the spectators' attention. Here suddenly the* vaqueiro *puts his head outside one of the arches, signaling his presence and announcing the ox's entrance. The choral singers start to sing the following wake:*

Look ox, look ox

Well, to the owner of the house

You are going to celebrate

Etc.

It was during the singing of this song that the vaqueiro *presented himself guiding the ox which now danced, now scattered the people, now assailed with his horns and which afterwards, fell down dead. Thus, in the circle of the dead ox the* vaqueiro *stomping and making faces tries to bring it back to life, singing:*

I went to see my ox,

Eh! Bumbá!

What did it have?

Eh! Bumbá!

Finishing this song, which is very much like a reminder, the ox gets up, shakes itself, and scatters the people with its horns, crowning the play with a song by the vaqueiro *who, throwing a handkerchief at me, received the usual tip.*[44]

I am certain that this is the *rancho* to which da Câmara Cascudo is referring when he writes that it "consists of a fusion of *reisados*, made up or not, which send praises to the Three Wise Men from the east, receiving gifts. Each one of these *reisados* or *rancho*, characterized itself with a symbol—animal, bird, star—and the group took the name of this sign."[45] Referring to the objective of Bumba-meu-

Boi in Henry Koster's writing to explain the absence of the play in the first decade of the nineteenth century, da Câmara Cascudo summarizes thus:

> *What appears logical is the existence of* reisados, *divided into* 'ternos [*threesomes*] *and* rancho,' *coming from representations of social groups in the procession of* Corpus Christi *and parades, during royal festive celebrations, commemorations of births and weddings of princes. Characters began to appear, and being bound together in a dancing nucleus initially, and after forming independent groups, came the singing, because there was no singing in official parade functions. A wooden framework, covered with a cloth, colorfully decorated and with the head of an ox, armed with immense horns, conceals a man who makes it move, turn and dance. The decorated framework is the center of interest of the Bumba-meu-Boi.*[46]

Alvarenga defines *reisado* this way: "The *reisado* is primarily a sung presentation consisting of a single episode, which succinctly contains the complete meaning of the subject." Continuing, the author concludes: "Given the brevity of these sketches, they were usually presented in series, and their sequence was guided by only one criterion: the final *reisado* was always the Bumba-meu-Boi."[47] As for the latter, the author asserts that "[it] consists of a series of independent scenes, characterized by the successive appearance of different characters, who dance or mime in response to a theme given by the song, ending with the death and resurrection of the ox."[48] Confirming the early version of Bumba-meu-Boi, Alvarenga continues:

> *Through a process of lengthening of popular creations, numerous episodes borrowed for the most part from another form of dramatic dance, the reisado, bound themselves to the theme of ox, and other popular scenes and types. The latter consisted of scenes of criticism of customs; one could find the satire of slave guards, priests, lawyers, judges, tax collectors, etc. Together it forms an enormous rhapsody, with a number of variants, the basic unity being maintained by the theme of the death and resurrection of the animal.*[49]

The above comments by Alvarenga are quoted in Meyer's article in *Revue d'Histoire du Théatre* (1963), where she supplements Alvarenga's writing by dividing the Boi into two episodes: a procession which begins with singing and dancing and announces the second part often called *ambassade*, often performed in front of a notable's home. Maria Isaura Pereira de Queiroz, who adds her own conclusion about the *reisado*, in turn shares Meyer's observations:

> *The* reisado*…is the most complex manifestation of popular theatre that we have. It is usually produced during the festivities of* Reis *[Kings] from which it derives its name. The procession runs through village streets or paths in the forest to receive monetary gifts or provisions, which will be used to organize the feast, and at the same time announces the time and locale where the festivities will be held. The farce, which is presented is composed of a series of short scenes revolving around the story of an ox. Whence the names it carries in different regions.*[50]

The above conjectures on the original version of the Boi in Brazil as expressed by de Melo, da Câmara Cascudo, Meyer, and Queiroz are best summarized by another conjecture by Borba Filho:

> *In spite of the prevailing common denominator in these descriptions, at its inception, Bumba-meu-Boi was unquestionably a sacred drama, a public* reisado *[merrymaking] based on the ox in the manger at the Birth of our Savior Jesus Christ. Little by little, other* reisados *were joined to the spectacle. The ox as a quasi-sacred animal was merged with the ox of the pastoral region, the profane invading the religious merrymaking.*[51]

In spite of the prevailing common denominator in these descriptions of the original form of the Boi—a religious event with a series of scenic frames—one is left with doubt. Is it possible that these authors are trying to find similarities in two events of different nature? While the *reisado* may be processional, the Boi has a theatrical concept that is definitive of and vital to the procession. It is like comparing an *Escola de Samba*'s parade to a *Maracatu*, which also has a parade section, but whose essence is not a dramatic reproduction of a legendary plot. In short, *Rancho do Boi* or *Reisado do Boi* is not Bumba-meu-Boi. Assuming that the former has laid the foundation for the latter, then we may logically suppose a transformation of the *rancho* or *reisado* into a powerful folk drama, such as Bumba-meu-Boi, whose plot is of Brazilian origin, as da Câmara Cascudo presents. It cannot be overemphasized in this work that Bumba-meu-Boi, as conceived in Brazil, is this plot, and by definition, the plot in question is the reflection of colonial Brazil in which the social interaction is displayed in the mantle of the ox.

CONCLUSION

By no means do I argue in favor of a non-diffusionist theory. However, in defining cultural practices one should be aware of the imminent danger with similarities, for they often lead to erroneous conclusions. Sometimes it is best to focus one's attention on why a manifestation is where it is, rather than assume, a priori, that it must have been borrowed from elsewhere. With Bumba-meu-Boi, one must examine the underlying conditions that led to its creation in Brazil before losing oneself in the myriad of theories presented in the foregoing discussion.

To recapitulate, there are several conflicting theories in regards to the origin of Bumba-meu-Boi and its nature. Guilherme Theodore Pereira de Melo (1947) sees Bumba-meu-Boi as a variant of Gil Vicente's sixteenth-century play *Monólogo do Vaqueiro*. Luis da Câmara Cascudo (1954) expands the above theory by deriving the Boi from Portuguese *Touradas*, although he maintains that the plot upon which the action of the Boi evolves is purely Brazilian.[52] Marlyse Meyer (1963), Maria Isaura Pereira de Queiroz (1913), and others shared Cascudo's thoughts relative to the origin of the Boi. Equally important in this European consideration of the origin of the Boi is Artur Azevedo (1906), who recalls the Parisian masquerade *Boeuf-gras*, reintroduced in France by Napoleon Bonaparte, and which, until the eighteenth century, traveled through the streets of Paris carrying song and dance from door to door in the manner of the Brazilian *ranchos* described by Pereira de Melo. Mário de Andrade's

African totemic theory (1934; 1935; 1937) is supported by Edison Carneiro (1937) and José Ribeiro de Souza (1970). Domingos Vieira Filho (1968) asserts that the enslaved African who performs it to celebrate the ox's heroism Bumba-meu-Boi was brought to Brazil. Further research can determine whether slaves added the religious devotion to Bumba-meu-Boi as a camouflage, a protective measure from authorities, as they have done to other cultural manifestations.

In the light of new evidence revealed by personal research, it can safely be concluded that Bumba-meu-Boi is an indigenous folk drama created by members of the lower social class, primarily Blacks, depicting the social interaction existing between members of the lower and upper social classes in colonial Brazil. To the members of the lower class, Bumba-meu-Boi was a means of denouncing slave owners and slave catchers during the colonial period. In the course of time, the basic structure of the Boi was expanded to meet other social needs, including criticism of unacceptable behavior regardless of social class. The examination of the structural organization of the Boi will shed further light on its *raison d'être*.

CHAPTER II

Structural Organization of Bumba-meu-Boi

Such scholars as Domingos Vieira Filho, Queiroz, and José Ribamar Sousa dos Reis have dealt with the structural organization of Bumba-meu-Boi perfunctorily. They rush conclude hastily Bumba-meu-Boi is a medium through which members of the lower class satirize the ruling class. However, often ignored is the fact that Bumba-meu-Boi also provides an opportunity for its participants to comment on their personal life, publicly criticize or sanction vices in the community, and expound upon news of communal interest. A closer examination of the subject matter developed in the dramatization of the death and resurrection of the ox reveals content directly concerning the Boi's evolution. It is formulated as both sung and spoken dialogue, spiced with humor and class satire.

The present chapter is divided into two sections. The first analyzes the Boi's dramatic structure. Equally pertinent at this level of analytical consideration is the detailed description of the internal organization of each constituent part. In order to expand the definition of the term "structure" to engender what is herein referred to as "total structure" of the Boi, the second part examines the social structure of the Boi in relation to the society in which it evolved. The analysis of the administrative structure is also relevant for illuminating the network of social behavior and the role fulfilled by leaders within the Boi.

THE DRAMATIC STRUCTURE OF BUMBA-MEU-BOI

Although the storyline of all Bumba-meu-Boi presentations is based on the legend described in Chapter I, there are variations deriving from regional interpretations of the legend and from the addition of local characters. Regardless of stylistic variations, there is only one major structure that is followed by all Bumba-meu-Boi presentations. Speaking of these internal sections at the roundtable debate, Américo Azevedo Neto explains the *guarnecer* (gather up), the *lá vai* (there goes), containing the actual presentation of the drama, and the *eu cheguei* (I have arrived) to acknowledge the venue where the performance is going to take place.[1] In his explanation, Américo seems to have left out the *despedida* (farewell) that is dramatized at the end of the presentation, especially in preparation of the ox's execution at the end of the season. For the sake of the present study we shall consider the version presented by the Boi de Zé Vale troupe, where the bulk of fieldwork time was spent. Bumba-meu-Boi dramatized by the Boi de Zé Vale troupe in Pindaré contained five sections organized to provide the merrymaking for which the occasion is intended while maintaining the underlying devotional atmosphere of the event. The sections are: (1) *Cordão*; (2) *Guarnição*; (3) *Cordão*; (4) *Matança*; (5) *Cordão*. Of the five sections, the legend is dramatized only in the *Matança*. The remaining four sections prepare and establish the atmosphere for the drama.

Cordão

Literally, the term *Cordão* means twine or string. Generally, in the Brazilian carnival, it refers to a group of organized merrymakers, but in Bumba-meu-Boi, *Cordão* identifies a dance format adopted by a troupe. Although similar in content and structure, each *Cordão* fulfills a specific function in the dramatic progression. For example, the first *Cordão* is a prelude to the entire event, during which musical instruments are tuned, final decorative touches are made to costumes, and the participants arrive at the site of the celebration. The second *Cordão* links the *Guarnição* and *Matança* sections, and the third reestablishes the joyful atmosphere of the celebration after the sadness of the *Matança*.

To begin, the Amo blows the whistle and sings the first *toada*, accompanying himself with his *matraca* (wood blocks). Participants learn the melody and lyrics by joining in as the Amo repeats the *toada*, which serves also as the refrain, and introduces the topic to be expounded upon in verses improvised by individuals around the circle. The accompanying musical ensemble begins its participation with the Amo's improvisation of the first verse. As they dance to the percussive ensemble's rhythmic tapestry, some members accentuate rhythmic pulses and others articulate the smallest note values in the rhythmic organization with *matracas* in their hands. The Amo or his assistant draw participants' attention and allows the next *toada* to be intoned by blowing of the whistle to mark the end of each song. The number of *toadas* sung during a *cordão* is determined only by time, since traditionally the fourth section of the Boi must start at one o'clock in the morning. The subject matter of the *toadas* and verses includes a variety of topics such as love affairs, sports, self-praise, commentary on current events, the beauty of the event at hand, and gossip. The ox does not participate in the first *cordão*, probably because it is still being decorated. According to Mr. José Vale, however, the ox does not partake in this *cordão* because Saint John has not blessed it.

Guarnição

The name *Guarnição* means gathering. It is a section composed of four segments, *guarnição, processão, apresentação, salve da reza*. The first of these, *guarnição*, from whence the name of the section is derived, begins with the gathering of the troupe outside the doorstep of the house where the ox is being adorned for the occasion. The Amo or the Patrão blows the whistle, summoning the group with the *toada*, "Toquei no meu Apito" (I Blew My Whistle).

REFRAIN:

> *I blew my whistle*
>
> *In order to gather up*
>
> *Oh! my Saint John*
>
> *Oh! come to bestow a blessing on us*

CHAPTER II

To deliver us from our enemies

From those who wish to conquer us

This *toada*, and others sung at this time, tell of the beauty of the gathering and invoke Saint John.

The gathering follows no specific pattern. As soon as the ox appears inside the house, the themes of the *toadas* change from calls to assemble to requests that the ox, seated on the floor, stand up.

REFRAIN:

Arise ox, the morning ox

With God and our Lady

VERSE:

Oh! Arise the King of Union

Oh! Arise from the cold ground

I want to lead you

To Saint John's altar

To keep a promise

Fulfill my obligation

Although several *toadas* are sung with the same request, the ox standing up does not constitute a segment, nor does the following phase in which the ox is asked to come out of the house. Structurally, these two phases provide a smooth transition from the first to the second segment of the *Guarnição* section.

REFRAIN:

Come outside ox

The hours are passing

I want to show these people

A tailed star shining there

VERSE:

Come outside ox
Come out into the grounds
Oh! see how beautiful it is
Say ox, my vaqueiro!
I am going to lead you to the altar
Of the patron Saint John

or

REFRAIN:

Come outside ox
There are more (people) who desire to see you
Saint John is waiting at the altar
To receive you

VERSE:

Come outside ox
Come outside into the grounds
I am going to lead you to the altar
With the patron Saint John
See how beautiful it is
Together with my companions

At the end of these two bridge-like phases, terminating with the appearance of the ox on the doorstep, the whistle is again blown to begin the second segment of the *Guarniçáu*.

CHAPTER II

Processão

The procession (*processão*) takes place between the house where the ox was being decorated and the shed where Saint John's altar has been temporarily erected for the occasion. Unlike the gathering, the procession follows a specific order. Three women precede the ox: Dona Maria (the Amo's wife) and her two assistants all dressed in white. Between the other two women, Dona Maria holds a framed image of Saint John in one hand and a tin can rattle in the other. The other women carry only a tin can rattle, which is shaken in a rhythm consistent with that of the entire troupe. Behind the ox comes the Amo with the Patrão, followed by the rest of the troupe. During the procession there is singing and drumming but the three women and the ox proceed calmly without dancing as they sing these songs:

REFRAIN:

I am going to lead my ox

Portrayed on a flag

Saint John is going right ahead

Guiding our path

and

REFRAIN:

There goes, there goes

There goes the ox for those who wish to see

I am going to lead the King of Union

Making the ground to tremble

VERSE:

I am going to lead the King of Union

With the patron Saint John

And see how beautiful it is

At the arrival into the compound

The third segment of the *Guarnição*, during which the *Apresentação do Boi no Altar* (Offering of the Ox at the Altar) takes place, begins with the same reverence as the initial gathering. Several things can happen during this phase depending upon the time of year. At the year's first presentation, June 23, the make-believe ox frame cannot be used in Bumba-meu-Boi until it has been baptized. This takes place at the altar. The baptism is performed according to Catholic ritual, including godparents who are obliged to give presents to the ox after the ceremony. After the first presentation of the year, baptism is no longer required and the ox is presented to Saint John with songs of offering. *Toadas* sung during the entire *Guarnição* section derive their themes from the constituent segments. The improvised verses, however, are more personal and directed to Saint John by individual singers. This is the moment when participants come to Saint John to keep their promises and thank him for all he has done for them during the year. It is also an opportunity for them to bring their grievances to the patron saint and to make new requests.

REFRAIN:

Saint John here is your ox
I brought it to you
I came to keep my promise
I came to fulfill my duty

VERSE:

Saint John here is your jewelry
It is I who brought it
I came to keep my promise
That the devout made

CHAPTER II

Saint John here is your ox

Oh! my patron saint

I came to keep this promise

Together with my companions

Oh! give me life and health

That I may sing in the entire world

The *Guarnição* section ends with the *Salve da Reza* (Round of Prayer) during which prayers are recited, and Latin and Portuguese religious songs invoking the Holy Trinity, the Virgin Mary, Saint Peter, Saint Paul, and others are sung. However, before starting this devotional phase, a short mock prayer is led by a Cazumbá who jokes with Saint John in *toadas* such as the following.

PRAYER:

Oh! My Saint John

Who is holding a lamb

Beware of José Vale

Because he is the best of thieves

He went to your ranch

And he is going to steal your cattle

There is also Dona Maria

Who is a loving spouse

Today she is mourning

Does not have joy in her life

Because it has not been three months

Since she lost her loving mother

Continuing this descriptive style, a *toada* is sung to announce the beginning of the prayer segment.

REFRAIN:

> *It is about time*
> *For those who wish to pray*
> *But, get down on your knees ox*
> *And cross yourself*

VERSE:

> *Kneel beautiful ox*
> *At Saint John's altar*
> *In order to receive the promise*
> *Fulfill your obligation*
> *After the promise has been kept*
> *It will rejoice my heart*
> *Kneel beautiful ox*
> *It is Saint John who ordered*
> *Kneel at the altar*
> *Waiting for the praying*
> *It is to keep this promise*
> *That the devout had made*

Praying is not mandatory. In Pindaré, most participants leave the premises during the prayer segment to have a drink outside the shed. Women and children composed the bulk of the audience participating in the prayer, and were led by the person portraying the Padre in the drama.

At the end of the *Salve da Reza*, everyone returns to the altar and the Amo requests permission from Saint John to take the ox outside to play.

REFRAIN:

> *Saint John has been prayed to*
> *The praying is done*
> *I want you to grant me permission*
> *For my ox to arise*

VERSE:

> *Saint John, I have already prayed*
> *Together with my companions*
> *I want you to grant me permission*
> *To lead the ox into the grounds*
> *This troupe is organized*
> *Speak to the ox my* vaqueiro!

and

REFRAIN:

> *I've already prayed*
> *To my Lord Saint John*
> *I've already arisen, I'm going to call*
> *My* vaqueiro's *attention*

VERSE:

> *Good night Saint John*
> *My true saint*

Give me life and health, Saint John

To me and to my companions

I am going to keep this promise, Saint John

In this Brazilian room

Oh! my Lord Saint John

Oh! give me life and health

Activate my memory, Saint John

That my singing does not change

If I should die singing Boi, Saint John

Cover me with your virtues

Now, with the ox blessed for the year, the second *Cordão* begins and the ox takes part, dancing inside the circle along with Cazumbás, Indigenous persons, and mythical characters, who tease it and run away as it attempts to attack them with its horns. This *Cordão* goes on until it is time for the *Matança*.

The above description illustrates that the functional value of the *Guarnição* is to establish the religious overtone that permeates this folk drama. *Guarnição* provides the opportunity for Bumba-meu-Boi participants and observers who have come with more than just the intent of having fun to direct their grievances to Saint John. *Guarnição* is also a section that establishes the setting for pious devotion amid this predominantly secular celebration.

Matança do Boi

The entire drama as related in the legend evolves during this section. *Matança* takes place in front of the shed where Saint John's altar is located. The Amo, Dona Maria, and the Patrão are sitting with their backs toward the entrance to the shed. In front of them are two rows, one of *vaqueiros* and the other of *rapazes* (young men, servants). Between these rows Pai Francisco and the ox stand and face the seated authorities. The first scene begins with the singing of the following *toada*:

REFRAIN:

The hour has come
For our ox to die

VERSE:

Appear, the First Vaqueiro
Get ready for my ox to play
Oh! Speak to the ox my Vaqueiro
At the gate of the corral
Oh! Speak to the ox my Vaqueiro
Don't let it hit you
Oh! Speak to the ox my Vaqueiro
Bring it from there to here
Oh! Speak to the ox my Vaqueiro
Let it know you
Oh! This ox has a habit
Before it is hit, it hits
Oh! My ox is a wild animal
It never learned to pray
Beware of this ox
Don't let it pierce you
Oh! This ox has sharp horns
It can pierce you

> *Oh! Withdraw yourself my* Vaqueiro
>
> *Searching your place*

The same *toada* and verses are repeated for each of the six *vaqueiro*s and six *rapazes*. The calling continues with the rest of the characters but with a different set of verses. The Patrão sings these verses to the Amo.

> *Oh! Bring the ox from there to here*
>
> *Beautiful (ox) that I want to see*
>
> *Oh! About face my master*
>
> *Searching your place*

Then the Amo sings the same for the Patrão and continues with the mention of other characters' names.

> *Oh! Appear the good Caboclo [Indigenous person]*
>
> *Get ready for my ox to praise*
>
> *Oh! appear Nêgo Chico,*
>
> *Catirina, Cazumbás*
>
> *Oh! Nêgo Chico, speak to the ox*
>
> *Bringing it from there to here*
>
> *Oh! Nêgo Chico, bring the ox*
>
> *From the fence of the corral*
>
> *Oh! My ox is into the grounds*
>
> *It is time for it to die*

After each character has taken his place, the killing of the ox continues with the second section of the *Matança* during which Pai Francisco is dared to kill the ox with this *toada*:

CHAPTER II

Chico, kill the ox

If you want to do it

The verses contain descriptive remarks of Chico's shotgun, praises of the beauty and strength of the ox, and directive words about how, where, and when Chico should shoot the Boi Estrela. The following are selected verses that deal directly with the content of the *toada*.

With this shotgun

You old black Cazumbá

Carry this shotgun

Without safety lock or holster

There comes the bull

It is coming breaking fences

There comes the bull

Scattering vaqueiros

Carry, Chico, carry

Aim and shoot lightly

Shoot at the Boi Estrela

At the heart's blood vessel

Shoot, Chico, shoot

Watch out don't miss

Eh! Chico pay attention

Shoot when I tell you

Shoot, Chico shoot

It is time to shoot

At the end of the singing Chico follows the Boi Estrela into the woods, aims and shoots. The third episode contains the announcement of the death of the ox by a *vaqueiro* returning from keeping watch on cattle in the field.

REFRAIN:

The ox has died

The Royal Fame has died

My Master's ox has died

And leaves sadness for crying

VERSE:

Being a poor vaqueiro

Wondering in the land covered with second growth

I found our ox

Dead from maggot-filled sores

Being a poor vaqueiro

Taking care of cattle in the field

I found our ox

Dead under the shadow of large trees

The fourth section of the *Matança* section of the Boi is a quest for the guilty person who has killed the Boi Estrela. Amo interrogates each of his six *vaqueiro*s and six servants to identify the killer of the ox. Here is the reproduction of the entire dialogue, where the Amo speaks and the responses are sung.

MASTER:

Eh! First Vaqueiro*!*

CHAPTER II

1ST VAQUEIRO:

People keep silence
I hear my master calling
I don't know if it is for good
I don't know if it is for bad

MASTER:

Eh! First Vaqueiro!

1ST VAQUEIRO:

My Master when you called
My horse was loose
I was sleeping and dreaming
That our ox was dead

MASTER:

Eh! First Vaqueiro!

1ST VAQUEIRO:

My master when you called
I was getting ready to come
The gate was closed
I could not get out
I heard trampling of the horse
And I came this way
I thought that it was my master
Who was coming after me

I heard trampling of the horse
And I heard knocking out there
I thought that it was my master
Who was coming to get me
Good night lord my master
How are you, how have you been
Here is your good vaqueiro
Why have you called
Good night lord my master
How are you, how have you been
Here is your good vaqueiro
For whatever you may need

MASTER:

Vaqueiro *saddle my horse*
Saddle even yours
I want to win the plea
That the giant did not win

1ST VAQUEIRO:

My master, don't you know
That your horse died?
It was grazing in the field
And the snake bit it

MASTER:

> Vaqueiro, *don't say such a thing*
> *That I become very angry*
> *If my white horse* [jurema] *is dead*
> *Then saddle my brown one* [rosto queimado]

1ST VAQUEIRO:

> *My master, don't you know*
> *That your English saddle is changed*
> *English saddle that saddles white horse*
> *Does not saddle the brown horse.*

MASTER:

> Vaqueiro *go there to my house*
> *There to my house on the veranda*
> *Go bring me my book of prayers* [livro mestre]
> *I want to win the argument*

1ST VAQUEIRO:

> *My master, I went to your house*
> *And looked around on the veranda*
> *I didn't find your book of prayers*
> *With which to conquer the plea*

MASTER:

> Vaqueiro *go there in the house*
> *In the smallest drawer*

Go and bring my book of prayers
Ink pot, paper, and pen

1ST VAQUEIRO:

My master, I went and came back
There in the smallest drawer
The inkpot was dry
I didn't find paper or pen
My master, I went and came back
None of these have I found
I found Dona Maria
And conversed with her

MASTER:

How annoyed I am today
I'll hit you with this iron rod
If the iron rod does not hurt you
Vaqueiro, you are right

1ST VAQUEIRO:

My lady, help me
My master wants to hit me
Because of our ox
Which didn't sleep in the corral

DONA MARIA:

Being Dona Maria,

CHAPTER II

Woman of great wisdom,
One does not mistreat a vaqueiro
On this ranch, I do not permit it
Kneel my vaqueiro
Kneel and ask forgiveness
I have a golden ring
For your freedom
Don't cry my vaqueiro
Your master will not hit you
I'll give him a hug
And he will forgive you

1ST VAQUEIRO:

My lady, tell me
That your vaqueiro *is beautiful*
Riding on my horse
With my little ribbon bow

DONA MARIA:

Vaqueiro, you are not beautiful
Because your master does not want
I have a little golden box
All covered with rings
Arise, my vaqueiro
Arise from the cold ground
I am Dona Maria

Your master's spouse
Arise, my vaqueiro
Go over there
To look for the ox
At the gate of the corral
1st Vaqueiro: *I kneeled with sadness*
But I have risen with happiness
There is a God in the heaven for me
And Dona Maria on earth

What follows is spoken dialogue.

MASTER:

Eh! First vaqueiro*!*

1ST VAQUEIRO:

Yes, master.

MASTER:

Eh! First vaqueiro, *where have you been?*

1ST VAQUEIRO:

I went to a party with Dona Maria and
I am arriving this morning. When you called
I almost did not hear you, but I was not very far.

MASTER:

Why do I have you on my ranch?

CHAPTER II

1ST VAQUEIRO:

For your protection.

MASTER:

What kind of protection is this that while coming through Campo da Gama, by the riverbank in the back country, I found our King of Union dead on the ground. Can't you tell me who killed him? Vaqueiro!

1ST VAQUEIRO:

No, master, I can't tell.

MASTER:

Even as news?

1ST VAQUEIRO:

Even as news.

MASTER:

Even as information?

1ST VAQUEIRO:

Even as information.

MASTER:

Even in dream?

1ST VAQUEIRO:

As a dream, I heard between the sky,

the cloud and the stars,

that it was the second vaqueiro.

MASTER:

Then call the second vaqueiro *for me.*

1ST VAQUEIRO:

Call him yourself, you who have big mouth.

MASTER:

What are you doing here?

1ST VAQUEIRO:

Oh! Second vaqueiro, *my master is calling you.*

MASTER:

Oh! Second vaqueiro, *why do I have you on my ranch?*

2ND VAQUEIRO:

For your protection.

MASTER:

What kind of protection is this that while
I was coming back through Campo da Gama,
by the riverbank in the back country,
I found our ox dead on the ground,
do you know who killed it?

2ND VAQUEIRO:

I do not know, master, because I don't sleep with the ox.

MASTER:

Not even as news?

2ND VAQUEIRO:

Not even as news.

MASTER:

Even as information?

2ND VAQUEIRO:

Even as information.

MASTER:

Even in dream?

2ND VAQUEIRO:

In my dream,
I think the third vaqueiro *has the information.*

MASTER:

Then call the third vaqueiro *for me.*

2ND VAQUEIRO:

Call him yourself, you who has a big mouth.

MASTER:

Oh! Vaqueiro, *don't answer impertinently.*

2ND VAQUEIRO:

Oh! Third vaqueiro, *my master is calling you.*

MASTER:

Oh! Third vaqueiro, *where have you been?*
I call you crying and you answer singing,
Third vaqueiro*!*

3RD VAQUEIRO:

It is because my master is sad and I am happy.

MASTER:

[Same dialogue as above]

3RD VAQUEIRO:

In my dream I heard that it was the fourth vaqueiro.

MASTER:

Then call the fourth vaqueiro *for me.*

3RD VAQUEIRO:

Only my master who has a tongue this big.

MASTER:

Yah! Call him for me.

3RD VAQUEIRO:

Oh! Fourth vaqueiro, *my master is calling you.*

4TH VAQUEIRO:

Here I am, master.

MASTER:

Oh! Fourth vaqueiro, *where have you been?*

4TH VAQUEIRO:

My master, I went sightseeing in the garden today, the palm trees were beautiful.
I was talking with Dona Maria, and I am arriving now.

MASTER:

Why do I have you on my ranch?

4TH VAQUEIRO:

For your protection.

MASTER:

[Same dialogue]

4TH VAQUEIRO:

In my dream, between the sun, the cloud, and the stars, I heard that it was the fifth vaqueiro.

MASTER:

Then call the fifth vaqueiro *for me.*

5TH VAQUEIRO:

Here I am, master.

MASTER:

Oh! Fifth vaqueiro, *a beautiful* vaqueiro *like you, why do I keep you on my ranch?*

5TH VAQUEIRO:

For your protection.

MASTER:

[Same dialogues until the sixth servant]

6TH SERVANT:

I don't know. The first servant knows.

MASTER:

I have asked all of you and nobody could tell me anything. The first vaqueiro *said the second knows, the second said that the third knows, etc…*
Sixth servant told me that it is you who knows this beautiful gang. Why was my ox killed?

1ST SERVANT:

They told me, master, that they were afraid to get in trouble, that is why they put everything on me.

MASTER:

Why didn't you tell this in the first place?

1ST SERVANT:

I was afraid of being punished.

MASTER:

Where the guilt goes, that is where the blame is placed, you see? So, you do not want me to know why my ox was killed?

1ST SERVANT:

It was not me sir. Sir, I am going to tell you.

MASTER:

Who killed my ox?

1ST SERVANT:

*You are not going to tell
where you received the information.*

MASTER:

No.

1ST SERVANT:

I think that it was Black Chico.

MASTER:

Right, Black Chico?

1ST SERVANT:

*Why then don't you go and get Black Chico for me.
That is difficult, as you know.*

MASTER:

Give him a message to come and deal with me.

1ST SERVANT:

I have told you that I don't know the way.

MASTER:

You don't know the way?

1ST SERVANT:

I don't know.

At this moment, the indigenous Chief is told to take his subjects, find Pai Francisco, and bring him back. Fearing for his life and those of his people, the Chief requests the Padre's benediction that is administered in a very humorous manner, bringing laughs from all those present. Leading the search, the Chief sings:

I am singing and crying

My master sent me

After Black Chico, my master

My ox is already dead

Singing and crying

Outside of this hole in the ground

After Black Chico, my master

With a flat nose

Singing and crying

On these paths

After Black Chico, my master

He is there in the corner

Singing and crying

My master sent me

After Black Chico, my master

My ox is already dead

[Speaking]

1ST SERVANT:

Good night, Mr. Chico.

CHICO:

Good night.

1ST SERVANT:

We have come to take you in now.

CHICO:

Now I won't go, I am curled up with my woman.

[Singing]

1ST SERVANT:

Good night, Mr. Chico
How are you, how have you been?
We have come to take you in, Chico
My master sent us

CHICO:

I was stretched out
In my orange grove
These damned dogs
Came to wake me
I was stretched out
In my orange grove

These damned dogs

Came to bother me

I was stretched out

In my banana plantation

These damned dogs

Came to wake me

I was stretched out

In my banana plantation

These damned dogs

Came to bother me

I was stretched out

On tangerine leaves

I was stretched out

Together with Catirina

The fifth section of the *Matança* begins when *Chico* is finally brought before the master to stand trial. The Master summons everyone on his ranch to witness what has happened and to mourn the dead ox:

Gather up, vaqueiros

On Saint John's Night

To mourn our ox, my vaqueiros

Don't let it fall to the ground

With a guilty look in his eyes, Chico sings out excuses to justify his action:

I was playing with the ox

But I didn't mean to kill it

The shotgun discharged itself, my master

And killed your Royal Fame

I was playing with the ox

Beneath the green branches

The shotgun discharged itself, my master

And killed the famed ox

I was playing with the ox

There on the hill

The shotgun discharged itself, my master

While falling out of my hands

In the course of his excuses, Chico does not miss the opportunity to insert some ironic remarks about the situation:

I requested a barrel to be made

Of the tin

In order to shoot this ox, my master

At the heart's blood vessel

I requested a barrel to be made

Measuring three fingers in diameter

In order to shoot this ox, my master

Right on the meat of the chest

I requested a barrel to be made

Of iron

In order to shoot this ox, my master

I want to see it lay on the ground

To these remarks, the master answers with curses and condemnation of Pai Francisco's act, and they carry on a dialogue:

MASTER:

The cursed big shotgun

Pai Francisco's shotgun

Where it shot the bullet, my vaqueiro

It looks like lightning

CHICO:

Yes, it is lightning

When it hits a tree

It burns a bluestem, my master

What would the wool from the lamb say

MASTER:

You can burn wool from lambs

Of these new born

But "of my ox you will not burn" Francisco

It is a jewel of our Lady

With Pai Francisco's confession, the trial ends and the Amo pronounces sentence to revive the Boi Estrela. Two Portuguese medical doctors and one indigenous healer enter the scene and approach the ox, which is lying on the ground. They each take turns attempting to revive the Boi Estrela. The doctor's attempts are in vain and finally the Amo's favorite animal is resurrected by the indigenous medicine man. At the sight of seeing his ox come back to life, the master invites everyone to rejoice with him in a final *Cordão*.

The end of a *boiada* season is marked by the singing of the *despedida*, a series of farewell songs directed to the ox's godparents and to one another. This moment is filled with sadness because most of the participants will not be seeing each other until the next season.

The basic structural organization of Bumba-meu-Boi can be summarized as an alternation of structured and unstructured or miscellaneous sections. In the structured sections such as *Guarnição* and *Matança*, *toada* subjects are prescribed by progressive phases of the presentation. They primarily describe the ox's and participants' actions. Likewise, verses improvised during these sections derive their content from the prescribed *toada* topics. Although the latter are the same each year, their melodic material varies from year to year or from one presentation to another. In the unstructured sections, *Cordões* (sg. *Cordão*), the subjects of the *toadas* are diverse and not descriptive of any particular action. Nonetheless, *Cordões* are the links connecting the basic elements of the Boi. They also are sections in which participants are given license to externalize their personal feelings about life and comment on aspects of life in their community and the world.

Wherever the Boi de Zé Vale troupe performs, the season of the Bumba-meu-Boi presentation has a distinct structure defined by the birth and death of the ox. At the first session, that year's symbolic ox is constructed. But for it to represent the troupe and be worthy of Saint John's acceptance, it must receive a Christian baptism to rid it of any evil spirit that may have lodged in its wood and to purify its "soul" so that it may bring peace and protection to the entire troupe during the year. The last presentation of the season is held on a date selected by the officers of the troupe. At this event, the ox, which had been resurrected by the medicine man in earlier presentations, is no longer curable and his death is irreversible. It is then destroyed and its meat symbolically distributed among members of the community (see Fig. 1). The length of time between the ox's birth and death varies from one troupe to another and from one year to another, based on the troupe's financial situation and the number of performance invitations the troupe has contracted for the year. The standard Bumba-meu-Boi season begins on June 23 and ends on January 6.

Meat distributor.

Blood Distributor.

THE SOCIAL STRUCTURE OF BUMBA-MEU-BOI

To understand the social structure of Bumba-meu-Boi is to unveil its *raison d'être*. In the previous chapter it became evident that Bumba-meu-Boi is not a cult of the ox, nor does its organization engender totemic implications. Certainly, Domingos Vieira Filho's thesis that Bumba-meu-Boi was a celebration of the ox by the slaves of colonial Brazil for having shared a common fate was also dismissed with impunity. In brief, Bumba-meu-Boi is a legendary folk drama attesting to the social interaction among different classes in colonial Brazil.

Those who believe that the origin of Bumba-meu-Boi is rooted in the Portuguese play *Monólogo do Vaqueiro* (1502), as evidenced by its observance during the Christmas period in the northeastern Brazilian states, may still wonder at an apparent contradiction: In Maranhão, the Boi is linked with a celebration of Saint John. The fact is different Catholic saints are honored in different parts of the country. For example, in São Paulo, the Nossa Senhora de Aparecida Day is an important religious event observed by people from miles around. They make a pilgrimage to visit the site of the apparition, pray, and renew their sacred bond with Nossa Senhora de Aparecida in the cathedral built in her honor. In Maranhão, Saint John is the most highly regarded saint. Although there are several regional saints, the Festa do São João (Saint John's Festival) is the most important statewide observance. It is celebrated in conjunction with São Pedro (Saint Peter) and São Marçal (Saint Mark), during the *Festas Juninos* (Festivals of the month of June). Although Saint John's prominence in Bumba-meu-Boi in Maranhão is unquestionable, participants also invoke Saint Peter and Saint Mark, as demonstrated in the following verse:

If I should die singing Bumba-meu-Boi

Saint John do my burial

Saint Peter, Mark, Mark

Cover all the expenses

"Why Saint John?" it may be asked. According to participants from different Bumba-meu-Boi organizations, there are two primary reasons. First, in an area where cattle-raising is as important as it is in Maranhão, this saint, sometimes referred to as *São João dos Carneir-*

inhos (Saint John of the Little Lambs) is considered the shepherds' patron saint. He is always portrayed with a lamb on his lap. The second reason, and probably the more important of the two, reflects the Brazilian concept of the godfather– godson relationship. The authority of the former is superior to that of the godson's biological father. Senhor Benedito Coreia, the *palhaço* (clown) in the Boi de Zé Vale troupe, says, "Saint John is godfather of Jesus. This role places him above other saints who only serve as intermediaries between God and the believer. They do not intervene on their own. This is not true of Saint John. Being Jesus' godfather, he need not request permission from his godson to grant a wish."[2] Consequently, most participants who are also *vaqueiros* have adopted Saint John as their personal saint, and the *boiada* is the perfect medium where they can be in direct communication with him to thank him for what he has done for them and to make new requests. From this perspective, Bumba-meu-Boi offers an opportunity to communicate with Saint John.

Several relevant questions come to mind at this point. Was the ox, around which the plot is built, selected on the basis of the reasons enumerated in the first chapter? Is this merrymaking associated with Saint John because of his importance in the lives of then Bumba-meu-Boi creators? Should the answer to these inquiries be yes, the definition of Bumba-meu-Boi resides in its two aspects: (1) secular and satirical, built around the ox; and (2) religious and reverent, centered on Saint John.

There is a diversity of reasons, collective and personal, religious and secular, that causes individuals to participate faithfully in Bumba-meu-Boi. The most common is to fulfill promises made to Saint John after a crisis in one's life. Of those responses I collected from the Madre Deus group in São Luis, one particular response illustrates this general concept:

> *Five years ago, I was driving home late at night after a long drinking session with some friends at the Olho d'Água beach. On my way, coming down the hill by the police headquarters, I made a false move and the car left the road and went into the ditch. Boy! I almost died. But I remember being in the Hospital Presidente Du-*

tra lying on my back and saying to my Lord Saint John, if you get me out of this alive, I promise to sing Boi for three years. I've kept my promise, but ever since I have been feeling so good, and my life is [so much] better now, that I wouldn't stop participating in Bumba-meu-Boi.[3]

Similar testimony was recorded by Prado in her master's thesis, "Ano Tem: As Festas na Estrutura Social Camponesa" ("It Is Held Each Year: Festivals in the Social Structure of the Peasant"). The husband speaks:

Last year the woman went to São Luis ill, and gave birth to four sons all dead. Then she made a promise to the Lord Saint John: if she became pregnant again and had a live baby, if it was a boy, at the age of fifteen he would participate in the Boi, and if it were a girl, I would participate. Comes the month of June, she has this baby girl, she is alive and I am singing Boi. I did all I could to keep this promise in that year…After eight years I am participating, but it is no longer to keep a promise. I sing because I want to. I am ready.[4]

As illustrated by these examples, an individual may participate in the Boi to keep a personal promise made to Saint John or one made by a relative or family member. There are those who sing the Boi because they enjoy it—some of whom have been involved in it since childhood. It is enlightening to observe two interviewee's eyes sparkle as they explain what Bumba-meu-Boi represents in their lives. After several difficult attempts to put into words what they feel about the Boi, they simply summarize, saying, "*Bumba-meu-Boi é a mais linda brincadeira*" (Bumba-meu-Boi is the most beautiful merrymaking). Relating what had happened to him the previous year, Senhor Manoel spoke with sadness, "*No ano passado eu não pude brincar porque estava muito doente. Oh! Professor, o que chorei foi muito por não ter participado na brincadeira*" (Last year I could not play because I was very ill. Oh! Professor, I cried so much because I could not participate in the merrymaking). Senhor José Vale, the Amo of the Boi de Zé Vale troupe, participates because "*a boiada é a única brincadeira que eu gosto desde que eu era menino*" (Bumba-meu-Boi is the only merrymaking that I have liked since I was a little boy).

Another reason for participation in Bumba-meu-Boi, discussed in a number of documents but not encountered among the Boi de Zé Vale members is economic, namely the wages paid to individuals by the owner of the Boi. According to Prado, there are those who participate because they have been invited and promised money by the owner for each presentation they take part in. This remuneration is derived from the amount of money received from a contract and distributed on the basis of the number of people with roles in the presentation. The high-ranking personnel, such as the Mandador or the Palhaço—song leaders who are sometimes referred to by scholars as spokesmen of the troupe—receive more than triple what the Mió-lo, the individual inside the frame of the ox, receives.

Joila Moraes reports another aspect of this phenomenon in her article, "O Bumba-meu-Boi de Axixá." In it, she writes:

> *The Boi de Axixá comes out every year during the festivities of the month of June, with a new ox which changes cloak and name from year to year. Participants' clothing is also changed every year. In this troupe, contrary to what happens in others, it is the organizers of the "merrymaking" who buy and make props for all participants, who are also paid for each presentation, varying the amount between thirty and one hundred* cruzeiros *per person according to the role he plays during the performance.*[5]

In Pindaré, the Boi de Zé Vale troupe is organized along a different set of financial arrangements. For each contracted performance, the president of the troupe, Senhor Armando, receives the agreed-upon fees and delivers them to the troupe's treasurer. These funds and the members' annual dues are kept for the following year's expenses, which include the purchase of the material for the ox's frame, the fabric for the *lombo do Boi*, ox skins for new drum heads, and food for troupe members during dress rehearsals and home performances. In addition, a percentage is retained to provide financial assistance to members during the year. This practice has been in the Boi de Zé Vale troupe for so many seasons that in 1981, when this data was recorded, there were improvised verses to this effect.

This is how the performance of Bumba-meu-Boi goes

At the arrival into the groups, Golden Jose

You are a friend of mine

You sing Bumba-meu-Boi, because you like it

It is not to make money

Each year, each year I sing in Bumba-meu-Boi

Oh! redhead, never have I made money

My pleasure is to sing to Saint John

He helps me so that I can drive cattle in the field

Although the monetary factor cannot be dismissed altogether in Maranhão, payment for participants is not a general practice. However, in 1972, with the advent of the *Federação e Centro de Defesa dos Grupos de Polclore do Maranhão* (Federation and Center for the Defense of Folklore Groups of Maranhão) operating under the charter of the *Impresa Maranhense de Turismo* (MARATUR), an organ of the state government under the secretary of tourism, registered troupes began receiving aid from the government. This aid is given in the form of materials for props, financial aid, and transportation to carry troupes to performance venues determined by the federation to be for the benefit of the public. In April 1978, a local newspaper, *O Jornal*, published an announcement made by the president of MARATUR, Senhor José Gomes Figueiredo:

> *Impresa Maranhense de Turismo has acquired (through an agreement with the Fundação Nacional de Arte of the Ministry of Education and Culture) help for the folklore ensembles of the state...particularly those of Bumba-meu-Boi [which] will have the opportunity to improve their garments and those of their participants. The help will include the necessary material such as* miçangas [*glass beads*], canutilhos [*small ornamental glass tubes*],

tapes and paetes [*shaggy woolen fabric*], *which can be acquired at MARATUR, by groups registered in the Centro de Defesa do Folclore Maranhense.*[6]

The owners of Bumba-meu-Boi, in spite of the fact that they express resentment over the small amount received, value this aid. Some of them recall the hardships they went through in order to organize a *boiada*. According to Senhor João Francisco do Espirito Santo, also known as João de Chica, owner of a Bumba-meu-Boi troupe, things are better now than they were in the past: "In former days the Boi had several owners, but each year one organized the *boiada*...The Boi has changed for the better, primarily in clothing." Senhor João Câncio dos Santos expressed the same idea in the same newspaper article: "Without help nobody can organize a Boi anymore. Today you can't spend less than three thousand *cruzeiros* ($743) to construct the frame of the ox."[7] Others, such as Senhor Laurentino Araújo, think that public performances requested by the government in exchange for the subsidy are a hindrance to paid contracts: "For years the government has been helping with a small amount in exchange for public performances. This does but hinders our chances, because sometimes there is an invitation somewhere for the troupe to make money."[8]

Fig. 2 The ox's farewell to the city.

In summary, the Boi holds great value for each person who participates, though reasons for doing so may differ. There is a strong feeling of devotion to Saint John, Saint Peter, and Saint Mark that is facilitated by communion through Bumba-meu-Boi. These participants believe in Saint John's power to perform miracles for his devotees, and the Boi can serve as a testament of a personal covenant. The ox, whose presence invokes the shepherd saint, is also treated with reverence. As it makes its farewell passage through the streets and paths, an atmosphere of sadness reigns over the town (see Fig. 2). At the last performance of *Matança*, several participants and observers cry at the sight of the dying animal as it staggers from Pai Francisco's bullet wound. Participants invest in the existence of the ox to such an extent that a member of the Madre Deus troupe in São Luis said, "Each year, at the *Matança do Boi*, we [symbolically] lose one of our members." Yet despite the power participants ascribe to the ox, the plot of Bumba-meu-Boi remains secular and carries the intent of social criticism. José Ribeiro de Souza sustains this assertion:

In the dramatic section, the sense of criticism is constant, often in a marvelously hidden symbolism. It comes up like a most perfect relief valve of the less favored population of Brazilian society. Around the ox, it takes the position against the prejudices and different wrongs of the social organism, ridicules the powerful and even the misfits of their own group.[9]

ADMINISTRATIVE STRUCTURE OF BUMBA-MEU-BOI

The network of relations that exists among participants of Bumba-meu-Boi has received little attention in the published literature. This omission frequently stems from the writer's ignorance of the vital role played by the administrative organization in the functioning of the troupe. These functional roles complement each other and assure the smooth operation of the troupe, strengthen its unity, and guarantee its continuity. Seen from this conceptual point of view, the administrative structure of the Boi mimics that of a corporation.[10]

Besides the character roles designated in the drama, Bumba-meu-Boi contains administrative positions that are held by troupe participants. A close examination of these positions will illuminate the essence of the network of social relations upon which the principle of solidarity of the Boi is built. An individual or a group within a community can establish a Bumba-meu-Boi troupe. As with its presentation, the founding of a troupe can be the fulfillment of a promise or simply an expression of personal preference for merrymaking. In either case, the founder holds the post of the president and the cofounders are called *sócios* (associates). The president signs contracts for private presentations and determines the performance schedule and fees (see sample contract below). Normally, the position of the president of the troupe is reserved for a male member, but some women have occupied this post in Maranhão troupes.

CHAPTER II

FOLHA DE CONTRATO

Nome da turma de Bumba-meu-Boi 'M Dourado' de Pindaré Mirim

Contratei com o Sr _____

uma noite de representação de Bumba-meu-Boi no dia _____

com as seguintes despesas: _____

ou sem despesa _____

residência em lugar denominado _____

a iniciar as ____ horas e encerrará as ____ do dia seguinte no justo valor de

Cr$ _____ cuja importância tenho que receber no encerramento da hora acima citada

                              Pindaré Mirim _____ de _____ de 19 ___

Testemunhas:

_____   _____
                                                  Contratante

_____   _____
                                                  Proprietário

CONTRACT SHEET

Name of the Bumba-meu-Boi troupe 'M Dourado' from Pindaré Mirim

Contracted with Mr. _____

One night of Bumba-meu-Boi performance on _____

With the following expenses: _____

Or without expenses _____

Residing at the following address _____

To start at ____ hours and end at _____ of the next day for the amount of

Cr$ _____ the total of which I have to receive at the end of the

Hour mentioned above.

Pindaré Mirim ____ of _____ of 19 ____

Witnesses:

_____
Contractor

_____
Owner

Illustration 1 - A sample of Bumba-meu-Boi booking contract
(Example from the 'M Dourado' troupe in Pindare, 1981)

Associates are responsible for naming the troupe. They decide on the name of their ox for the season and determine the *sotaque* to be adopted by the troupe. They select the site which will serve as the troupe's headquarters, set the date for the *Matança*, and acquire permanent props such as Saint John's portrait and supplies for making the frame of the ox and its cloak. The associates' responsibilities include recruiting members and feeding the troupe at rehearsals and local presentations.

The majority of Boi troupes visited in São Luis and in Pindaré have a *director de tripulação* (crew director) who is responsible for discipline during rehearsals and performances, especially those occurring away from home. This is an aspect on which outsiders judge the troupe. The position of crew director is a very sensitive one, because he has to deal with individuals who are under the influence of alcohol for the duration of the gathering. His treatment of participants can work in the troupe's favor during recruitment of members. The Boi de Zé Vale troupe takes such pride in its treatment of participants that there is a *toada* that denotes this factor.

REFRAIN:

José Vale's troupe

Oh! has been blessed by Jesus Christ

It is a strong established troupe

Which does not mistreat singers

You wish to see what cattle rustle's roar is

Go to Antenor's small ranch

To avoid alcohol abuse by participants during the gathering, and to establish an equal distribution of the communal beverage, there is a *distribuidor de cachaça* (rum distributor). At the performance, rum is distributed during the *Cordão* and during the procession in the community (see Fig. 3). Each participant waits his turn as the distributor makes the rounds, serving everyone from the same glass.

Fig. 3 Rum distributor.

Whoever plays the Amo role in the drama, he may also be the leader of songs, called the *mandador* (song leader). He directs rehearsals and actual presentations of the Boi assisted by the *palhaço* or *contre-Amo*. He assigns roles to individuals, has the authority to invite individuals to participate in the Boi, and can exercise the authority to expel anyone who does not behave properly at the *boiada*. The Amo designates the successive order for the intonation of *toadas* and can stop any *toada* that does not observe the prescribed poetic rules. Often the troupe's name contains that of its Amo, such as Boi de Zé Vale, Boi de Apolonio, etc.

Although responsibilities such as the embroidery of the ox's cloak and the construction of its frame are non-administrative, they should also be mentioned because they are considered honorary responsibilities. The former is fulfilled by a woman, a member's spouse, who receives the necessary material from the president and embroiders the design representing the theme for the year and the name of the troupe on black velvet with pieces of mirror, beads, and other colorful and shiny objects. These are important responsibilities because the worth of the troupe—artistic and monetary—is judged by the physical appearance of its ox. Women may work diligently for six months to create an artistically beautiful cloak. The frame is constructed by a male member of the troupe or by a hired contractor.

However, the final touches before and during the presentation are completed and maintained by the women.

A mutual respect prevails between leaders and other members of the troupe. Each individual takes pride in his responsibility to strengthen his group and protect its honor. Authority held in the Boi is extended into the community. As their leader, the Amo is sometimes looked upon as a powerful godfather. He is often asked to resolve quarrels between members and to attend to their personal problems.

In light of these observations, it is reasonable to agree with Prado's deduction that Bumba-meu-Boi has a corporate structure with internal rules of solidarity that create specific rights and obligations for its members. These rules of solidarity are corroborated by the tradition of competition between groups. This was one of the reasons why the performance of Bumba-meu-Boi was prohibited in Maranhão. This prohibition is discussed in detail in Chapter IV.

CHAPTER III

Sotaque: Styles and Stylistic Changes

Since its first presentation in the eighteenth century (ca. 1780) during the so-called Civilização de Couro (Leather Civilization) era, Bumba-meu-Boi continued to evolve by adapting to changes in the social fabric in spite of persecution from civil authorities. The argument for enslaved African authorship of this folk drama presented in the first chapter need not be recapitulated here. This is sustained by several facts, primarily the function for which the drama was created and the sequence in which its various styles appeared.

In Maranhão, there are three major styles, each of which reflects characteristics peculiar to each of the racial groups that compose the Brazilian population: the African style called Boi de Zabumba, the indigenous style known as the Boi de Matraca (dated to 1868), and most recently Boi de Orquestra, introduced in 1958. Each group brought its own interpretation to the rhythmic organization, costumes, dance presentation, and choice of musical instruments. The latter two styles imitated the African by maintaining the play's storyline and its dramatization without necessarily adhering to the original purpose. Each of the new styles incorporated features reflecting the ethnic identity of their respective groups. Over time, as its original functions became obsolete, modifications to the religious overtones and a shift in the application of community-focused social control became critical to Bumba-meu-Boi's survival.

SOTAQUE: STYLES

Sotaque is a term used to refer to the variety of styles of Bumba-meu-Boi in Maranhão and Piauí. According to Américo, interviewed in

São Luis, July 7, 1986, *sotaque* is analogous to regional accents (i.e., differences in the pronunciation of Portuguese spoken in São Paulo, Rio de Janeiro, Maranhão, and Bahia). Américo's assertion is corroborated in Maranhão by the presence of three *matraca* styles: Boi de Pindaré, Boi da Ilha, and Boi de Viola, which appeared in São Luis after 1999. Although the three styles utilize wood blocks and *pandeiros* (hand drums) for their primary rhythmic patterns, they differ in the size of these instruments and in the overall tempo. Whereas small *matracas* and *pandeiros* are used in Pindaré, larger sizes are standard in Ilha, thus modifying their names to *matracão* and *pandeirão* to reflect their larger sizes. In Boi de Viola, on the other hand, *matracões* and/or *pandeirões* are combined with the ten-stringed guitar and an occasional harmonica, varying the Sotaque Ilha with the introduction of the viola. These peculiarities are apparent in the choice of musical instruments, costumes, tempo, and choreography which reflect the regional uniqueness of each style,[1] which in turn derives its name from the most prominent instrument in its accompanying musical ensemble, as in the cases of Boi de Matraca and Boi de Zabumba, or from its general musical instrumentation, as in the case of Boi de Orquestra.

Instrumentation

In spite of the style, the basic instrumentation of *batuque* (accompanying musical ensembles in Bumba-meu-Boi) is the same. It is composed predominantly of percussive instruments. The *matraca* is a pair of rectangular wood blocks varying in size from twenty to thirty centimeters in length by five to seven centimeters in width and two to three centimeters in thickness. Sometimes *matracões* (larger wood blocks) have a shallow groove carved down the middle of each façade, which amplifies the sound when the two blocks are struck together. During the presentation of the Boi, the player often secures *matracas* by a string around his neck, preventing himself from dropping and losing them. All participants who are not involved in the actual *bateria* play *matracas*. As personal instruments, each individual player according to his own criteria for size, weight, and decoration normally makes *matracas*.

During the performance, *matracas* fulfill the function of the timekeeper. They are hit one against the other to emphasize the basic timeline, often in duple meter and/or the variants of this, stressing the density referent. To begin a *toada*, the singer establishes the tempo by playing a measure or two of the *matraca* rhythm. As the rest of the troupe members join in the singing of the *toada*, their attention is given to lyrics, melody, and the *matraca* pulses established by the cantor. The crispness of their *matraca* performance is a measure of the troupe's homogeneity as an ensemble and weighs considerably in the evaluation of the presentation.

The musical ensemble in the Boi de Matraca style also contains a collection of hand drums varying in size from twenty to thirty centimeters in diameter, called *pandeiros*. A *pandeiro* is a single-headed frame drum covered with snakeskin or goat hide. In the José Vale troupe in Pindaré, all *pandeiros* as well as other drums within the ensemble, with the exception of the friction drum, are covered with snakeskin. As in the *bateria* of the *Escola de Samba* (samba school), the *pandeiro* stresses the triplet rhythmic patterns in the ensemble. The body is made of plywood or carved out of a tree trunk. Regardless of the type of material used to make it, the *pandeiro* used in Bumba-meu-Boi is far lighter than the industrially made *pandeiro* associated with *Escola de Samba* that has a metallic body and sympathizing metal discs. Other drums in the *matraca* instrumentation include the *bombo* (a double-headed bass drum) larger than the *pandeiro*, covered with snakeskin and played with mallets, hands, or a combination of the two. *Bombo* sizes vary from forty to sixty centimeters in diameter with frames generally carved out of tree trunks and adorned with geometric figures, flowers, or birds painted in various colors. There can be an unlimited number of *bombos* within an ensemble, all of which contribute to the emphasis of the binary pulse by playing in unison on the first and the third beats in a four-four rhythmic organization.

Another prominent musical instrument in this accompanying percussive ensemble in the Boi de Matraca style is the friction drum, which changes its name according to the cultural context in which it is used. In popular music, the friction drum is commonly known as *cuíca*, in *maracatu* it is called *porco* (pig), and in Bumba-meu-Boi it is called *tambor onça* (wildcat drum) (see Fig. 4). Its body is a hollowed-out tree trunk and its head is covered with goatskin, in the center of which is a shaft attached from the inside. Considering its internal shaft, the drum's origin is unquestionably African.[2] The rhythmic tapestry of the Boi this drum provides syncopated patterns, highlighted with a drowned sound imitating the roar of a wildcat or the bellowing of an ox.

Fig. 4 Tambor onça (friction drum).

Although a *matraca* is usually played by participants outside of the actual accompanying musical ensemble, in a number of troupes observed in São Luis and Pindaré, the Amo plays *maracás* (tin can rattles). Dona Maria and her assistants also play these instruments. The *chocalho*, a cowbell with a flap, is played by Cazumbas who provide contrapuntal rhythmic patterns peculiar to their clowning character and their offbeat dance steps (see Fig. 5). The total musical orchestration is completed by pea-whistles used by the Amo to direct the event and by Cazumbas to contribute to the animation and the ambiance. Finally yet importantly, a participant blows the tin can horn to imitate the bellowing of the ox.

Fig. 5 Cazumba.

In the Boi de Matraca style, one distinguishes two sub-styles differentiated by slight modifications in the size of their musical instruments and in the overall tempo. These sub-styles are the Boi de Pindaré, described later in this chapter, and the Boi de Ilha, differing from the first by incorporating larger hand-drums known as *pandeirões*, large-size *matracas* called *matracões*, and by adopting a faster tempo than that of the Boi de Pindaré (see Fig. 6).

Fig. 6 Boizinho Barrica.

The instrumentation of the Boi de Zabumba style is also composed primarily of percussive musical instruments. The principal instrument, the *zabumba* (see Fig. 7), is a cylindrical, double-headed drum with ox- or goatskin on both heads. Originally the body of the *zabumba* was made from a carved tree trunk or from plywood. Today metallic barrels are being substituted for these materials. In its original form, the skinheads were attached to the body of the instrument by wooden rings; in the modern version, metallic ones replace these wooden rings. However, the tuning system for both versions remains the same—tightening the rope or the bolts joining the two head rings. The *zabumba* is usually played in a fixed location, with the weight of the instrument resting on a peg.[3] During the procession, the *zabumba* is hung on a stick and carried on the shoulders of two persons while a third plays it freely.

Fig. 7 Zabumba.

The origin of this instrument and its association with Bumba-meu-Boi are still unknown. However, despite the lack of supporting evidence, some attribute the *zabumba* to Africa. Similar assertions about African cultural traits in Brazil should be dismissed for failing to specify the African cultural area of the alleged origin, and for failing to tell us about changes that might have occurred during a given period, leading to the attained structures, functions, and form of expression in the new milieu.[4] Padre Lopes Gama confirms only that the *zabumba* was first introduced into Pernambuco during the second half of the eighteenth century.[5] He does not mention the purpose for which the instrument was introduced nor does he include suggestions about its origin.

The ambiguity of the *zabumba's* origin centers on its name and morphologic structure. On the one hand, the structure of its modern version resembles that of the bass drum in the European musical tradition. But what must be kept in mind is that this new version is derived from a process of substitution of construction materials. On the other hand, the original structure of the *zabumba* is more closely related to the array of double-headed drums encountered in several West African cultures. In Nigeria, for example, there is the Atete drum from Ogun State, which is used for the veneration of Òrìsà during Egungun festivals.[6] This drum is used also during social gatherings.[7] It can be conjectured that the *zabumba* is an African instrument that found its way to Brazil, primarily in conjunction with the Yoruba religious practices concentrated in the area of Bahia-Pernambuco since the eighteenth century.

Similarities can be drawn between the inclusion of the *zabumba* in Bumba-meu-Boi and that of the *cuíca* or friction drum whose origin and inclusion in popular music are also ambiguous.[8] In short, the same principle can be applied here. Although the *zabumba* may have come from Africa, its survival in Brazil was made possible because this instrument—or another with similar morphological structure—was already known to members of slaveholders and the policing force prior to their arrival in Brazil. One need only examine studies of musical instruments with African origin in Brazil to be convinced of the number of instruments no longer in existence in Brazil because members of the ruling class were unfamiliar with them and could not find new musical functions for them. This is the case, for example, with the *chihumba* (bow-lute) from southern Angola, described in northern Brazil in the late eighteenth century by Alexandre Rodrigues Ferreira in his *Viagem Filosófica...1783–1792*, as *viola que tocão os pretos* (the small guitar played by Blacks).[9] Another case in point is the *mbira* or *sanza*, observed in Brazil in the first half of the nineteenth century by Jean-Baptiste Debret, who called it *marimbas*.[10] Neither of these instruments could substitute for any functions fulfilled by the guitar or its ukulele-like derivative, the *cavaquinho*. On the contrary, it is only to the *cuíca*, an instrument used in the invocation of the dead among the Bantu people, for example, that Brazil's ruling class members have attributed the carnival functions of their *sarronca*, a Portuguese indirect friction drum with an external friction stick.[11]

The *zabumba* varies in size, ranging from sixty to eighty centimeters in diameter and thirty to forty centimeters in depth. The body is painted in solid colors or adorned with geometric figures and other decorative motifs. Tuning is accomplished by tightening the rope holding the two rings around the drumheads. The number of *zabumbas* in an ensemble is unlimited. They provide, simultaneously, straight beats and variations of these, with heavy low-pitched tones that drown out the voices of the singers, and can be heard for miles around.

Other musical instruments included in the Boi de Zabumba style are similar to and carry the same names as those in the Boi de Matraca style, with the exception of the *tambor onça* that is often omitted from the *zabumba* style. The *pandeiros* are smaller in the Boi de Zabumba style than in the Boi de Matraca and Boi de Ilha styles. Some participants play these as they dance around the circle to emphasize contrapuntal triplet rhythmic patterns against regular beats of the *zabumba*. The *pandeiros* are tuned by warming up the skin-head of the drum with fire (see Fig. 8) or by placing them in the sun for a considerable length of time. *Maracás* are also played by a number of participants during the execution of the dance to stress the density referent.

Fig. 8 Tuning of pandeiros.

The Boi de Orquestra style derives its designation from the instrumentation that is predominantly melodic, harmonic, and of European origin. In contrast to the other styles, the musical ensemble of the orchestra style is composed of a combination of wind, stringed, and percussive instruments. The wind category includes trombone, trumpet, and saxophone, each of which plays the melodic line or harmonizes it heterophonically. The stringed instruments—guitar, *cavaquinho*, and sometimes the mandolin—underline the *toada's* harmonic structure with chord progressions strummed to the basic rhythmic patterns of the *boiada*. Among the percussive instruments are *pandeiros*, similar to those in the other two styles, the *bombo*, *maracás,* and some *chocalhos*, also equivalent to those found in other styles. The instrumentation of the Boi de Orquestra style also includes the *tambor onça*, which fulfills similar functions to those described in the Boi de Matraca style.

Music

The *Boi de Zé Vale* troupe in Pindaré, which contributes to the core of the present study, belongs to the *Sotaque de Matraca*. Its music is dominated by the extensive use of the *matracas* that provide the density referent played in improvisatory fashion by two interlocking timeline patterns of two against three (see the musical transcriptions in the appendix). Other musical instruments in the accompanying ensemble are the *tambor onça* that marks the main pulse in duple meter, often in 12/8, establishes the tempo, and gives the distinct character unique to the music of the merrymaking. The *pandeiro* derives its timeline patterns from those of the *matracas*. The *agogo* and cowbells with clappers played by the *cazumbas* reflect the disorganized choreography of their dance movements around the ox in the middle of the circle. The tin-can *maracás* subdivide the main beats to accompany the singing. As a percussive ensemble, there is only one accompaniment for all songs. However, the rhythmic tapestry provided by the ensemble is what Meki Nzewi calls *melorhythm* in that it is the product of multi-pitched percussive instruments (see illus. 2).[12]

SOTAQUE: STYLES AND STYLISTIC CHANGES

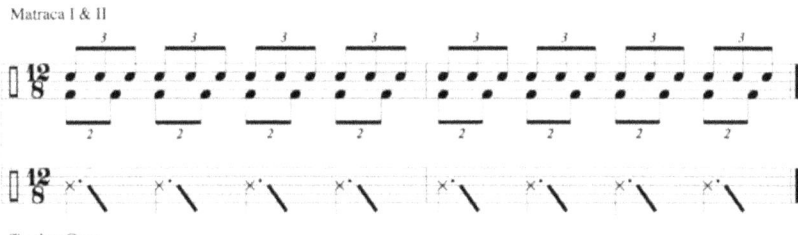

Illustration 2 - Transcription of the Bateria

CHAPTER III

Costumes

The designs and materials used in the costumes worn by dancers, musicians, and special characters that compose a Boi troupe constitute a significant stylistic distinction in Bumba-meu-Boi. There are several elements common to all the styles such as the black or navy blue velour cloth used as the basis for the dancer's *peitoral* (a sleeveless jacket), the *saiote* (a small skirt), and the *lombo do boi* (the ox's skin/cloak). Other common elements are the *missanga* (glass beads), *canutilho* (glass tubes used to decorate women's costumes), mirrors, ribbons used in the embroidery of motifs, figures and iconographic reproductions on the *peitoral*, and the *lombo*. There are pronounced differences, however, among the styles of performers' hats, jackets, and skirts.

In the Boi de Matraca style, dancers' hats are derived from the basic straw hat commonly worn by workers (fishermen, bricklayers, *vaqueiros*, farmers, longshoremen, etc.) within the state of Maranhão. For the Boi, the brim of the hat is enlarged with black velour cloth and reinforced with wire to accommodate the weight of the decorations sewn to the brim of the finished product. The velour cloth surface of the hat is then adorned with designs selected by the owner of the hat. These designs commonly depict a motif with religious symbolism, such as a church, Saint John with a lamb, and the like. These motifs are then surrounded with flowers, birds, and more to complete a scenic representation. On the rim of the extended portion of the hat are fixed feathers from the Ema bird (i.e., from the three-toed ostrich) of varying length, which greatly increase the actual size of the hat. At the lower back of the hat are sewn ribbons with geometric and flower designs of various colors. The ribbons are long enough to cover the back of the wearer and reach his thighs or ankles, depending on individual preference. The finished hat in this style weighs up to twenty kilograms. During the entire performance it is secured with the help of a string tied under the performer's chin.

The predominance of feathers in the Boi de Matraca style is accentuated in the costumes for the *caboclos* (indigenous people). The lavish costume for the Caboclo Real (Royal indigenous person) is made with feathers from the same birds as those used in the hat. This costume includes a hat, a skirt, shoulder and chest pieces, armbands, wristbands, and ankle bands. They are constructed of fabric totally covered with feathers (see Fig. 9). The children playing indigenous persons wear costumes similar to those of the Caboclo Real but theirs are not fully covered with feathers.

Fig. 9 Caboclo real (royal indigenous person).

There are also several types of hats worn in the Boi de Zabumba style, but the largest hat worn by the dancers best identifies the latter. This hat is made of the inside of a young *babaçu* (palm tree) branch, sewn into a traditional formal top hat shape and reinforced with wire. The hat is covered with ribbons similar to those on the Boi de Matraca hats, which hang from the top center all around the hat, leaving a space of about ten centimeters in front for the face. This interval is secured by a dome-like additional piece sewn to the hat and adorned with geometric patterns, stars, and so forth, as desired by the individual.

Hats worn by other dancers in the *zabumba* style and by the *zabumbeiros* (*zabumba* players) are made from the common regional straw hats covered with black velour cloth and decorated again with designs according to individual preference, elaborated with colorful glass beads. Still another type of hat is found in the Boi de Zabumba style. This is basically a straw hat to which is sewn a front piece, similar to the dome-like piece on the larger *zabumba* hat but which is even larger in size. On it are depicted motifs with colorful glass beads, and its back is covered with ribbons hanging from the top center of the hat to the individual's thighs.

There are some feathers in the *zabumba* style, especially among indigenous characters. The latter's hats may have a small amount of feathers, but the majority of hats for little indigenous persons are made of cardboard covered with glossy, colorful paper and topped with synthetic raffia. According to Mr. Laurentino, these synthetic materials have been infiltrating the Boi because the authentic materials are becoming scarce.[13] In the case of the feathers, for example, the Ema bird has been declared an endangered species by the government and can no longer be killed for its feathers. Consequently, the feathers used today for indigenous persons' costumes, especially by troupes in São Luis, come from different birds or are made of paper.

The *peitoral* of the *zabumba* style has a different cut than that of the *matraca* style. Unlike the latter, it is more like a cape. Its normal size stretches from the neckline to mid-forearm, extending two to three centimeters lower in front and back. The hem is finished with glass beads. The *saiote* of the *zabumba* style also differs from that of the *matraca* style in that it lacks side openings. Both the *peitoral* and the *saiote* are made of black velour cloth hemmed with glass beads and decorated with flowers and other motifs in glass beads. Uniforms are worn underneath the *saiote* and the *peitoral*. In a well-dressed troupe, these uniforms include a long-sleeved white shirt, red pants, and black shoes covered with white spats in the style of the military police.

The Boi de Orquestra costume also presents unique features. The basic costume is comparable to that of the Boi de Zabumba style: long-sleeved white shirt, red pants, black shoes, and white spats. Both the *saiote* and the *peitoral* are smaller in size than those of the *matraca* style. The *peitoral* measures about twenty to twenty-five centimeters from the shoulders to the waistline in front and back. The hat, on the other hand, is shaped like a papal hat and is reminiscent of *congaceiro* hats. It is made of straw or cardboard and is totally covered with colorful glossy paper or with black velour cloth decorated with glass beads. The ribbons complete the design in a manner similar to those used in the Boi de Matraca style. Unlike costumes in the other styles, the costume design in the Boi de Orquestra style is the same for all participants.

Choreography

The fourth category of stylistic distinction focuses on choreography, including dance movements and presentation format. Beginning with the latter, it is apparent that each Boi style has adopted a specific structure for the formation of the *cordão*. In the Boi de Matraca style, the basic format has dancers facing into the center of a circle and moving sideways in a counterclockwise direction. Musicians face in the direction of the dance movement. The indigenes, the Cazumbas, and the Ox dance freely inside the circle. In the Boi de Zabumba style, the circle structure is maintained only for the dancers who face and move in a counterclockwise direction, with the indigenes, Cazumbas, and Ox also dancing freely inside the circle.

The *pandeiro* players and the *zabumbeiros* stand outside the circle providing the musical accompaniment. The Boi de Orquestra style presents a totally different organizational pattern for the *cordão*. Here the *cordão* is a rectangle with the musicians on the shorter sides and the rest of participants occupying the two longer sides. All participants face the inside of the rectangle and dance in and out of it.

Basic dance steps for each style also present certain peculiarities in pattern and in stress. The *matraca* style dance is executed by moving three wide steps sideways to the right and three narrow steps back to the left. The directional move is completed with a lifting of heels before starting the movement in the opposite direction. Both the dance steps and the heel lifting are synchronized to the *matraca* strokes, which, as mentioned above, stress the density referent of the rhythmic organization.

The *zabumba* style dance, on the other hand, tends to be faster walking movements synchronized to the *pandeiro*'s strokes, and at times, the dance becomes more running than walking. This style of dancing is more physical and strenuous than the more reserved *matraca* style. The Boi de Orquestra dance style is closer to the Boi de Matraca style, but is even more restrained in its movements and is sometimes referred to as the "gentlemen's dance." The dancers move four steps forward in a zigzag pattern and repeat a similar motion in reverse to regain their original positions. There are hardly any outbursts in movement, such as jumping or running, as is encountered in the *zabumba* dance style.

The above analysis of the components of Bumba-meu-Boi provides a framework for the quest for norms of stylistic creations from which stem the stylistic distinctions. Each style is derived from the interaction of the legend, which is maintained as the unifying element, with features derived from extrinsic forces, usually the cultural-racial backgrounds of their participants. It became evident in the course of the analysis that such stylistic elements as the musical instruments, costume designs, and dance choreography are strongly influenced by, if not deriving their basic structure from, the three basic racial groups which first interacted at the creation of the Brazilian society. A strong indigenous influence cannot be ignored in the Boi de Matraca style, ranging from the *matraca* as its most prominent musical instrument to its metronomic meter pulse, the predominance of feathers as part of the costume design and decorations, and the choreographic patterns of the dance steps.

The African influence can surely be detected in the *zabumba* style through the morphological structure of the drum by the same name, and also through its heavy-sounding strokes. Little if any African influence can be found in the dance of the Boi de Zabumba style, which contains *gingas* (movements) similar to those of the *Tambor de Crioula* dance, with its periodic spins and physically strenuous movements.[14] Jeovah Silva França expresses the Africanness of the Boi de Zabumba style: "It is marked by the presence of the rumbling of the rustic percussion, profoundly felt by its followers like a distant echo of African drum beats heard at night in the houses of Mina rooted here...."[15] The European influence is apparent in the Boi de Orquestra through the musical instruments employed.

STYLISTIC CHANGES

Instrumentation

The coexistence of the three Bumba-meu-Boi styles in Maranhão dates to 1958. The testimony of the majority of older participants and that of the recorded documents on the subject point to the Boi de Zabumba as the first style identified there. "The first Bois on the Island [São Luis]," writes Cyro Falcão, "were called De-Zabumba-Tambor. Their history developed alongside the drum implanted here by the African."[16] The exact date of its consecration as a style remains still academic. However, it also became identified at a later period with the district of Guimarães, once a major slave center; thus the expression Boi de Guimarães is sometimes used in referring to the *zabumba* style.

It was only in 1868 that the first mention of the *matraca* was made in conjunction with Bumba-meu-Boi in Maranhão. João Domingos Perreira do Sacramento writes: "In this year's frolic they introduced the *matracas* sound with the accompaniment of dull shouts, which shivered bodies to hear them, without a minimum recollection of such things having been used in Bumba-meu-Boi."[17] In spite of this historical confirmation of the Boi de Matraca style in Maranhão, nothing is mentioned about the troupe that introduced this instrument. Nonetheless, this style is identified today as Boi de Pindaré and as Boi da Ilha, referring to the region of Pindaré Mirim and the island of São Luis, where it has attained a prominent stylistic identity. Recently, a new style appeared—Boi de Viola—in which the ten-stringed guitar is added to the island style.

Boi de Orquestra is the newest of the three styles and the only one for which all circumstances of its creation are documented. Mr. Francisco Naiva, also known as Chiquinho, founded it in 1958 in the city of Axixá. According to some, the orchestra style came into being when a group of band musicians was trying to accompany a Bumba-meu-Boi troupe after a rehearsal. Although this style is comparatively new, its influence is felt in the growing number of troupes performing it within the state, primarily in the cities of Rosário and Cavaco.

As a social entity, Bumba-meu-Boi has also been subject to forces of change within the milieu where it evolved. Although the original form of its presentation remains unknown to us, much has been written about the composition of the musical ensemble that accompanied the performance. As for the musical instrumentation and costume designs in Bumba-meu-Boi, study of the evolution reveals tremendous changes over time. With the advent of the orchestra style and the stylistic identification with its European instruments and cultural background, these changes are also noticeable in *toadas*, which seem to reflect cultural traits of these racial groups in melodic structure, rhythmic implication, and vocal production. Jose de Jesus Santos points this out:

> *Like with all folkloric manifestations, Bumba-meu-Boi has been suffering, in the last decade, in Maranhão, profound and curious modifications, from apparel, invaded by plastic and nylon, to songs, where the rhythm, especially in the Boi de Orquestra, is sometimes as a* baião [*a form of rhythm and dance in Northeast of Brazil*], *a samba, or almost as a yeh-yeh-yeh.*[18]

No standardized combination of musical instruments existed for Bumba-meu-Boi troupes. Each region—not only in Maranhão, but also elsewhere—exhibited peculiarities in this domain. Some of these instrumentation combinations continue to be used where stylistic distinctions comparable to those in Maranhão have not been introduced. In Pará, for example, Carlos Rocque records the following instrumentation in the musical ensemble of Bumba-meu-Boi in Amazon: "The orchestra is composed of a small guitar, ukulele, rebec, a cowbell and slats which animate and cheer all gestures, turns, strikes, and skirmishes of the ox, which dances here and there."[19] Dulce Martins Lamas writes of a different instrumentation combination he observed in 1965, in Belém, the capital of Pará. "The instrumental," he writes, "is composed of guitar, ukulele, tambourines, *tamborim*, and rattle, which accompany melodies composed specially for the presentation."[20] Gustavo Barroso records still another version of instrumental combination in 1949, writing about Bumba-meu-Boi in Fortaleza, Ceará. The author points out that the accompanying musical ensemble was composed of clarinet, guitar, small guitar, accordion, *zabumba*, and tambourine.[21] Alceu Maynard Araújo summarizes this aspect of Bumba-meu-Boi as follows:

> *Membranophones are the fundamental musical instruments of the Bumba-meu-Boi in the North and Northeast, and in the South it is the accordion, harmonica, or bagpipe. In Piauí, in the past* matraca *and pea-whistle were used, but today there are tambourines, drums, rattles, and friction drums. The pea-whistle has persisted while the* matraca *has disappeared. In Ceará, besides the harmonica, there are drums, ukelele, tambourines and* pratos [plates used as percussive instruments in old versions of accompaniment for schools of samba]. *In Recife, Goiania and Paulista,* zabumba, canzá, *small guitar, rebec and tambourines. In Santa Catarina, tambourines, bagpipes, snare drum, and guitar. In Rio Grande do Sul, only the accordion.*[22]

Since this was written in 1973, several changes have occurred in the instrumentation of musical ensembles in Brazil's Bumba-meu-Boi. In an article entitled "Boi-de-Mamão Catarinense em Disco" (Boi-de-Mamão of Santa Catarina State on Record), for example, the author indicates that in the state of Santa Catarina the accompanying musical ensemble of the Boi-de-Mamão combines tambourines, *tamborim*, accordion, and guitar. In six years the instrumentation has dropped the bagpipe and the snare drum.

According to Padre Lopes Gama's description of the 1840 Bumba-meu-Boi in Pernambuco, the dancing and singing were accompanied by small guitars and tambourines. Since then, changes have occurred that reveal regional preferences by (1) the addition of new instruments, mostly percussive, as encountered in most Bumba-meu-Boi outside of Maranhão; (2) the introduction of wind instruments; (3) the addition of more stringed and percussive instruments as seen in the Boi de Orquestra style in Maranhão; or (4) the total avoidance of melodic instruments and reliance solely on percussive instruments for accompaniment, as in the cases of the Boi de Matraca and the Boi de Zabumba styles, which are also in Maranhão. Delving a bit further, Padre Lopes Gama's description of the musical ensemble is a further confirmation of the fact that all three styles of Bumba-meu-Boi in Maranhão originated and evolved within the state following introduction around 1838.[23]

Music

Over the years, the musical style in vogue at any given period in the community can create changes in instrumentation and overall phrasing. In spite of these changes, the music of Boi maintains its characteristic flavor and continues to influence as often as it is influenced by the country's popular music. Such styles as rock-and-roll—often referred to as the "yeh-yeh-yeh"—have dominated the music of the Sotaque de Orquestra. This influence can be heard in the song "Quando Anoitece" that was immortalized by the Boi de Axixá.[24] Of all the changes that have occurred in the musical rendition of the Bumba-meu-Boi, none equals the music of a newly introduced variant of the Sotaque Ilha called Boi de Viola, exemplified by the *Boizinho Incantado* troupe. With new instrumentation, the music of this variant has acquired a different character, one similar to that of popular music. The differences lie in compositional techniques, vocal rendition, and the harmonic implication; in the past songs, the refrain and verses were improvised by all participants, but today this practice has subsided. The following music examples of Mandarins, Bailarino das Areias, and Coração da Beira Mar are transcribed from the *Bailarino das Areias* compact disc by the Boizinho Incantado in São Luis, Maranhão.[25] These songs are well-structured compositions by individual composers and recordings by professional singers who lead with verses while the rest of the troupe functions as a chorus, replying with the refrain.

Costumes

Little historical information sheds light on the costumes worn by Bumba-meu-Boi participants during the performance of the Bumba-meu-Boi in Maranhão or elsewhere. Nonetheless, it can be assumed that whatever these costumes were in the early days of the Boi, they evolved to their present designs. In Maranhão, this aspect of the production arrived after its introduction into the state. This is what Cyro Falcão writes:

> *The costumes for Bumba-meu-Boi originated with the encounter between all northeasterners who came to search for the wealth and pleasures of Maranhão. The black velour cloth and the glass beads [reminiscent of Maracatus] arrived with Piauíans and Bahians. The hats with feather brims and shining colors are of Pará-Amazon origin. There was also a Parnaiba hat similar to Lampião's cabra.*[26]

In 1944, Francisco Curt Lange photographed a Bumba-meu-Boi presentation in Recife, Pernambuco. In his pictures, reproduced by Mario de Andrade in his "As Danças Dramáticas do Brasil" (Dramatic Dances of Brazil), it is evident that the usual costume of the period was plain and simple without embroidery or colorful decorations. Musicians, for example, are shown wearing white pants and long-sleeved white shirts.[27] By 1955, specific designs for participants' costumes were becoming articulated. Since then, changes taking place in the Boi have emanated from various social and economic factors. For example, the scarcity of raw materials strongly influences the costumes. This is particularly evident in the feathers used abundantly in the Boi de Matraca style and sparingly in others.

Today, feathers are scarce and thus costly; nylon products or paper feathers are usually substituted for real ones.

Annually rising costs have prompted several major changes, including substitutions in costume materials and reduced ornamentation. "One of the major problems that Bumba-meu-Boi confronts in Maranhão today are these high cost of glass beads and the velour with which the ox is decorated."[28] This is one of the reasons for which the Imprensa Maranhense de Turismo created the Federação de Defesa de Folclore do Maranhão: a channel through which Bumba-meu-Boi troupes are assisted with these costly decorative materials and other aspects of vital importance to their survival.[29]

Changes in various aspects of Bumba-meu-Boi in Maranhão have stimulated certain degree of awareness and controversy among participants. There are those who believe that changes are inevitable, and they welcome and promote them in their own troupes. Others lament certain changes and welcome others. Mr. Apolonio Melonio, a prominent leader of a Bumba-meu-Boi troupe in São Luis, is quoted in a local newspaper:

In the interior of the state, Bumba-meu-Boi is performed more at ease, the vocabulary is different and funnier. Here, because of this [city] behavior, it has lost 20 percent of the Boi's happiness. Bumba-meu-Boi has changed now in our Baixada, due to financial hardship and the difficulties of life.[30]

Mr. Melonio is lamenting about social changes resulting from an urban social setting as opposed to the rural setting where he first experienced the Boi. São Luis, the city in which these changes began and continue to occur, offers a cosmopolitan surrounding in which outside influences easily permeate local traditions. The inevitability of change in Bumba-meu-Boi is best expressed by Canuto Santos, who says, "In the past, the amusement of Bumba-meu-Boi was all made with vinyl-coated paper. Today we have changed to glass beads. What is worst is that we cannot go backward."[31]

Speaking on these stylistic changes in the Boi for *O Estado do Maranhão*, Mr. Leonardo Martins Santos, founder of the Boi da Liberdade troupe, expresses his interest in promoting changes in certain aspects of the Boi in order to avoid monotony. To illustrate, he points out that the inclusion of the pea-whistle, first introduced by Mr. Euclides, brought the event under the control of leaders in such matters as stopping of *toadas*, which was impossible to do in the past.[32] Another improved aspect, continues Mr. Martins Santos, is the change of the ox's hide from one year to another. This practice, introduced by Mr. Gurutil in the district of Cedral, is in essence a further dramatization of the legend, which ends with the killing of the ox and the distribution of its meat. The logic behind Mr. Martins Santos's action is that if the ox is dead and the meat distributed, then everything associated with it should also vanish. This reasoning endorses the change of names at the baptism of the ox, symbolizing its new identity. With the new name comes a new hide with new iconographic representation.

Mr. Gurutil's intention, which has become the *modus operandus* of Bumba-meu-Boi troupes everywhere, has been stretched to an extreme. Today, a well-dressed troupe makes at least two hides for its ox per year. Joila Moraes indicates this phenomenon in the Boi de Axixá when she writes, "Bumba-meu-Boi of Axixá appears each year during the festivities of the month of June with a new ox which changes hides and names from year to year."[33] A similar situation is also encountered in the Boi de Madre Deus troupe where two to three hides for the ox are made each year.[34]

Props

The iconographic reproduction on the hide carries the year's essential theme, and depicts cultural and geographical scenes that reflect the troupe's surroundings, such as the loading docks at Itaqui in Maranhão or a representation of a vision experienced by the troupe's leader. Some of these are summarized by Cyro Falcão in his writing about the so-called "Bois Históricos" in Maranhão, on whose hides are depicted such matters as national arms, flags, Tiradentes, scenes of the first religious mass celebrated by a priest, the discovery of Brazil, the shout of Ipiranga, and the teaching of catechism to the indigenous people.[35] The sheer magnitude of cultural material on these hides is beyond the scope of the present work, and will be pursued in a later study.

In spite of his enthusiasm for changes in Bumba-meu-Boi, Mr. Leonardo Martins Santos also expresses regret for those changes in musical renditions of the Boi. "Bumba-meu-Boi has changed a lot, primarily in costumes. But that means that I think that it is better now—it is more colorful, richer. Only that it is becoming different in rhythm because these people here have more influence. They are not like the old timers."[36] Mr. Santos's regret certainly corroborates that of José de Jesus Santos expressed three years earlier.[37]

Participation

Changes of a different nature affect Bumba-meu-Boi. These changes have attained such acceptance within communities and troupes that they have become common practices. Consider female participation, which at one time was prohibited. In the past, all female roles, such as Dona Maria and Mãe Catirina were played by male participants dressed as women. Today, practically all Bumba-meu-Boi troupes in Maranhão assign these parts to females. What is also noteworthy here is the fact that the army of indigenous persons in the drama is assigned to young girls. In Belém, Dulce Martins Lamas observed:

> *Another point worth making here is the presence of actual females in Parasen Bumbas. Besides the character Catirina, which is played by a male in "women's clothes" who is also encountered in Bumba-meu-Boi in other areas of the country, in the state of Pará young girls appear as the ranch owner's wife, his daughters and peasants.*[38]

Social phenomena also had a strong impact on the conceptualization of the interpretation of Bumba-meu-Boi. As a result, several items were added, modified, or omitted in an attempt to improve or adapt this merrymaking to the period in which it was performed. As a product of human behavior, Bumba-meu-Boi is always adapted to the social setting and period of its performers. The latter formulate norms by which their behaviors are governed and continuously subject these norms to further modifications, to adapt them to new spatial and temporal surroundings. These social forces engender a battery of political, economic and religious phenomena; in the present situation, one is compelled to also include the forces of nature. What is abundantly available today may become scarce tomorrow if humankind does not know how to budget its usage, for human activity upsets the environment faster than nature has been able to within the same time span.

CONCLUSION

It is within the boundaries established by these guidelines that the present chapter is developed to (1) define the existing styles of Bumba-meu-Boi in Maranhão, and (2) analyze changes in style leading to the present stylistic expression by highlighting forces that have contributed to their molding. These stylistic changes result chiefly from material and social conditions, to be discussed in the following chapter. These changes assured Bumba-meu-Boi's persistence in the state of Maranhão; persistence which will, in time, assure its continuous acceptance and assimilation. In the following chapter, attention is given to the process leading to these phenomena, and to the effect of forces that influence societal thought *vis-à-vis* Bumba-meu-Boi.

CHAPTER IV

The Assimilation of Bumba-meu-Boi in Maranhão

The process of assimilation for Bumba-meu-Boi in the state of Maranhão is analyzed here from a historical standpoint. The focus will be on the rise and fall of the Boi as evidenced by its conflicts with arbitrary moral values established by the ruling class, its conformity to these values, and its eventual status as the most representative cultural expression of the state. For this quest, supporting evidence will be derived primarily from available local chronicles printed between 1858 and the present, supplemented with field data.

Elsewhere I maintain that a cultural element's continuity in society is a validation of its persistence in and assimilation into the society.[1] Although persistence and assimilation are not synonymous with continuity, they are conditions, *sine qua non*, for the fulfillment of the latter. This order of events is best comprehended when *assimilation* is a status awarded after the completion of the process of cultural exchange. Thus, assimilation is the advanced stage of the acceptance of a cultural element, and a stage at which continuity is initiated, while persistence guarantees the latter's evolution.

It is only at the stage of assimilation that one may begin to speak of the continuity of a cultural element in new surroundings. Until then, there are phases of cultural exchange, and each of which presents a chance for an element to be eliminated before its possible assimilation into the tradition. These phases include: (1) taking or creating a cultural inventory, allowing members of different origins or social classes in an emerging society to discover what they have in common and establish cultural common denominators which might become features of their culture; (2) evaluating the common denominators according to socioeconomic, moral, and geographic values to determine their compatibility in enhancing the lives of their users; (3) reinterpreting those elements that have been judged compatible to the new milieu by attributing to them new functions, as they gradually reach their point of assimilation.[2] The essence of this theoretical observation is applicable to the evolution of Bumba-meu-Boi in Brazil prior to initiating its process of continuity. These theoretical stages will become evident in the course of the discussion.

There are several reasons for Bumba-meu-Boi's persecution in Brazil. One of these, often referred to in the literature, is Bumba-meu-Boi's identification with slaves, whose humanity and moral values were not accepted by the ruling class. In its early versions, the Boi was characterized by sometimes-fatal fighting. The primary cause of these fights is often ignored in the discussion of this topic.

As a social group, a Bumba-meu-Boi troupe represents a cultural community, often defined by the local industry or simply by geographic or administrative divisions such as a district, township, or neighborhood. In the interior of the state of Maranhão one encounters communities in which industries such as fishing, cattle raising, agriculture serve as means of existence. In Pindaré, for example, the population derives its sustenance and identity from agriculture (inherited from the colonial period when the community was built around sugarcane mills and rice industries), small-scale fishing on the Mirim River and the neighboring lakes, and cattle raising, also inherited from the days of sugarcane plantations. These people take pride in being from their community and in participating in its local economy. This sense of belonging, especially in the interior of the state, until recently, is strengthened by minimal population mobility. A Bumba-meu-Boi troupe, a social group *par excellence*, reflects this phenomenon of cultural identity. This feeling of belonging is strongly underlined by Souza: "Members gather pennies, make tremendous sacrifices to maintain and demonstrate their existence as a group which thinks, acts, reacts and feels."[3] Consequently, they protect that which belongs to them, or that to which they belong, from outsiders' criticism and ridicule. Thus, verbal insults constituted the tradition for which public confrontations among Boi troupes were renowned. Prado states as much:

> *This code of alliance in a relation of confrontation, be it rivalry, or conflict, transforms itself into an expression of violence. Therefore, there are two types of violence that a Bumba-meu-Boi presentation can engender, depending on the considered enemy. Among equals, it is a 'contest of rivals'; among different classes, it is an object of repression activated by the dominating rule....If in the most restricted sense, the* boiada *[cattle] represents original communities, it can turn, itself, in a broader sense, into a language of defense of interest in an interclass confrontation.*[4]

Expressing similar thoughts from a different perspective, Souza also notes, "Bumba-meu-Boi arouses in its participants the feeling of existing as a cultural group, which expresses its opinion about other entities."[5] Each group boasts about the beauty of its ox and that of its community, acclaims its organization, and exalts the quality of its accompanying musical ensemble, while denigrating those of others. They do so in *toadas* and verses improvised according to prescribed poetic rules of the *boiada*.

The confrontation first took the form of verbal *desafio* (challenge), whenever troupes encountered each other in public places. In the Amazon region, Eduardo Galvão records such an encounter:

> *When Bumba-meu-Boi troupes encountered each other, members engaged themselves in a poetic challenge of improvised verse and dance movements. A Boi from a small town was once ridiculed in such a four-line verse:*
>
> *There comes the Boi*
>
> *Behind the pepper plant*
>
> *Never have I seen an [ugly Boi]*
>
> *Such as this from Itapereta.*[6]

Frequently members who could not formulate stronger or more satirical responses did not tolerate these mockeries. Invariably these verbal challenges ended in physical ones aimed at the destruction of the opponent's ox. This tradition of rivalry was not unique to

Bumba-meu-Boi in Brazil. It was also a common practice between *capoeira* groups and samba schools, which for similar reasons received the same treatment from the ruling class in their quest for recognition as cultural expressions that emanate from an authentic Brazilian cultural nucleus. "*Na capoeira,*" explained Mestre Noronha in Salvador, Bahia, "*quando o pau comia, a gente usava o próprio berimbau para se defender*" (In capoeira, whenever the fight started, we used the *berimbau*—a musical bow—itself to defend ourselves). In Bumba-meu-Boi, clubs, knives, and other objects were hidden under the ox's frame with the same objective in mind. *Sambistas* also used their musical instruments as defensive weapons.

From the Amazon region, we have the account of an anonymous citizen who expresses his resentment of Bumba-meu-Boi performance in the city:

> *I would like those men, who promised twice to turn away Dr. Rego of the police department, to come and see the disdain and isolation in which their protégé is held; they should come to witness his madness; they should also come to assist the presentation of the least deserved merrymaking for an authority, such as Dr. Rego practiced in the night of June 29, placing himself in front of a group of scamps with their 'Bumba-meu-Boi,' designating places where they were to dance, and had the impudence to threaten with prison a group of young men from the best city of Obidos, only because they were throwing small spools on directors of the bumba, who were his slaves Casemiro and Claudino.*[7]

In the same year, *A voz Paraense* published an article in which the author urges authorities to banish Bumba-meu-Boi from the city.

> *The Boi Caiado, celebrated on the vesper of Saint Peter's Day, by more than three hundred blacks, mulattos and whites, of different sizes, who late at night trampled the rocks and grasses of the streets and squares in the city and countryside, resulted in stabbings and blows with sticks besides shouting that was offensive to moral decency and public security. Let us hope that those responsible in the police would put an end to the Boi Caiado in a similar manner*

that Judas was finished with on the alleluia Saturday.[8]

From these opinions and others in reference to the state of Maranhão, it can be asserted that the banishment of Bumba-meu-Boi by the slaveholding and policing class was based primarily on social and moral issues, which constituted the secular character for which Bumba-meu-Boi was renowned.

Remarks relative to this assertion are chronicled in Maranhão newspapers since 1858. In this year, a short notice appeared in *O Globo* announcing the reappearance of the Blacks' merrymaking called "the Ox," which years ago the police had prohibited, considering it uncivilized. Three years later, the São Luis newspaper *O Imparcial* published a statement by an author who called himself Um Amigo da Civilização, "A Friend of Civilization":

> *When a large portion of the population takes upon itself to end with those firecrackers for being deadly, an authorization is granted to the stupid and immoral merrymaking of slaves called Bumba-meu-Boi, the reason for the firecrackers. It is even astonishing that this is still happening, when years ago the president ordered the police to no longer authorize this merrymaking, for being opposed to good order, to civilization and to morals. When, because of Bumba-meu-Boi, there are beatings with clubs and even stabbings, it is because of the enormous racket that breaks the silence disturbing the quiet needed to sleep, the silence that the police should maintain. We hope that the police reconsider the thoughtless step it has taken, and be responsible to public opinion for what may happen because of the Bumba-meu-Boi.*[9]

This rather strong statement invited in the same year a reaction from a columnist of the *A Verdadeira Marmota* newspaper, also in São Luis, who could not understand the reason for the prohibition of the Boi in his state. In his column, the author states that these negative reactions against Bumba-meu-Boi were due to the population's ignorance of the story behind the merrymaking, and concludes his column with a succinct description of the plot. Nevertheless, 1861 was the last year Bumba-meu-Boi was presented in Maranhão until

CHAPTER IV

1868, when its return was hailed in *Samanário Maranhense* by João Domingos Pereira do Sacramento.

> *In the last fifteen days, from June 12 to the present, this columnist has noticed a wise resolution by the police authority about the rebirth of an old practice, which seems to have been prescribed by our customs...Hurray! for the police and viva the Bumbá!...The columnist requests permission from those civilized spirits who have so much to fear for the rebirth of our old customs, to shout hurray! to Senhor Dr. Morato and viva the Bumbá.*[10]

In spite of this acclaimed return, Bumba-meu-Boi was far from being accepted in Maranhão. The return did not end the antagonism, but marked the beginning of its denouement, which occupied a considerable time span, herein referred to as a "period of tolerance." This period lasted nearly a century: from 1868 to 1965, the year when the first public competitive parade of Bumba-meu-Boi troupes was organized in São Luis. In this time, an atmosphere of both sympathy for and hostility toward Bumba-meu-Boi emanates from the published announcements. In 1869, for example, the newspaper *Paiz* published a letter requesting the chief of police to deny permission to Bumba-meu-Boi troupes even for rehearsal. Three days later, *Publicador Maranhense* published still another letter to His Excellency the Chief of Police, referring to the letter in *Paiz*, and pleading to the authority to grant authorization to Bumba-meu-Boi to appear that year:

> *On the contrary, we remind everyone that this merrymaking has always been held each year, and that even last year, it ran through this city three times without causing these cases mentioned in the Paiz. We hasten to request to His Excellency Mr. Chief of Police to act for the good and grant the permission to this merriment, which, taking place only once a year, does not incommode the good society, since some old slaves participate with their master's permission. This is one more guarantee for this distraction of the good youth. His Excellency, thus, in virtue you will attend to our request.*

ONE FOR MANY.[11]

As the period of tolerance neared its end in 1965, printed notices in newspapers seem to reflect a decrease of the antagonism against Bumba-meu-Boi in Maranhão and in other northeastern states of Brazil. Presentation of Bumba-meu-Boi could then be tolerated by the ruling class when it was held in closed areas designated by the police. "In Fortaleza [Ceará]," writes Barroso, "from about 1900, police allowed the Bumba-meu-Boi in closed areas."[12] In Maranhão, newspaper articles support the claim that this tolerance was not felt until early in the second half of the twentieth century. Until then, physical abuses were still occurring during confrontations between troupes. In 1915, an article entitled "Polícia que Dá e Apanha" ("Police Who Beats and Is Beaten"), appeared in *A Tarde*, containing an account of an event that occurred at the presentation of the Boi in the township of Mocajutuba. On that occasion there was a physical confrontation between the policeman and a participant of the Boi, because the former's brother was hit by a rock thrown during the merrymaking. On July 2 of the same year, an anonymous letter to the editor was made public in the same newspaper under the title of *O Boi*. It requests the intervention of the editor to the authorities to limit the space where the presentation of the Bumba-meu-Boi could be held:

> *Mr. Editor of A Tarde,*
>
> *It seems incredible that in a capital such as ours, the police would allow the famous "Bumba-meu-Boi" to roam freely in the main streets from nine o'clock at night until ten o'clock the next morning, as has been happening.*
>
> *This merrymaking (if such name should be given to this) should be permitted only in secluded areas; it is not right, it is not lawful nor proper that one observes such a sad and depressing event which lacks description.*
>
> *What awful times!*
>
> *Intervene for us, Mr. Editor, because it is already the time for the police to rise from the sleep.*

Some readers.[13]

Similar types of requests must have been brought to the attention of the authorities, leading to the restriction of Bumba-meu-Boi's mobility in the city. This is revealed in "A Morte do Bumba-meu-Boi" ("The Death of Bumba-meu-Boi"), an article published in *O Globo* forty years after the above letter to the editor. The author prefaces his lament with astonishment of what he reads in the paper:

I am reading in newspapers that it is prohibited for Bumba-meu-Boi groups to parade in the streets of the city, in demonstration of their characteristic dances, which will only be permitted in the suburban perimeter starting at the corner of Getúlio Vargas Avenue and Senador João Pedro Street. This is sad, you know? It is sad for us that people of Pernambuco, Alagoa, and Rio de Janeiro would learn that it is a crime to celebrate a tradition in the streets of the city of São Luis in Maranhão...oh! you, cosmopolitan city, that denies what is the most native in the veins of your people, I feel pity for you! for dark is the future of he who denies his past.[14]

The author continues with an invitation to Maranhense authorities to follow the example of their colleagues in other major cities such as Recife in Pernambuco, where during the festive period, *maracatus* are subsidized by the mayor's office and permitted to roam the streets of the legendary city. Maceio, Alagoas, during the month of Congada, the government helps buy clothing and other objects for the *lanceiros* to assure the continuity of this folkloric expression in the chronicle of Maceio. In the middle of Rio de Janeiro, Saint Barbara's Day is celebrated by the police in uniforms, and members of the local religious sects go to Copacabana beach to deposit flowers and gifts to the queen of the sea Yemanja, singing, "*Saravá!*" "In the near future," concludes the author, "it won't be necessary anymore to prohibit them [Bumba-meu-Boi troupes] from entering the streets. São Luis which had plenty [of cultural manifestations] will become the land which also had the most famous Bumba-meu-Boi in Brazil."[15]

Throughout this period of tolerance, which can also be rightfully called of "period of adjustment," one observes that certain practices such as physical confrontation were no longer observed. Bumba-meu-Boi troupes from different localities could now dance in the same place without incident. Today, in the Boi de Zé Vale, elder members still recall these events in their *toadas*:

REFRAIN:

I blew my whistle

In order to gather

Oh! my Saint John

Oh! come to bestow a blessing on us

To deliver us from our enemies

From those who wish to conquer us

As with samba, acceptance of Bumba-meu-Boi also began with the parade contest. Likewise, the samba's acceptance was indicated in 1917 with the recording of "Pelo Telefone," the first song with the official title of samba, and again in 1932 with the organization of the first public parade contest which established the *Escolas de Samba* carnival tradition of the Praça Onze in Rio de Janeiro, organized by the newspaper *Mundo Esportivo*. Praça Onze is the historic location where carnival's first competitive parade was organized in Rio de Janeiro. On July 13, 1965, the first Bumba-meu-Boi parade contest in São Luis similarly marked a moment of acceptance. The result of the latter was published in the July 17 issue of *Diário da Manha*. Of the fifteen Bumba-meu-Boi groups from the capital and the interior that participated, the newspaper published the names and places of origin of only the troupes winning the top three places. First place went to Turma de Pindaré (Pindare Troupe) from Floresta; Abafador da Ilha (The Island Muffler) from the quarter Maracana, São Luis; and Cooperação do Povo (People's Cooperation) from the quarter of Madre Deus in São Luis. Second place was taken by Conquistador (The Conqueror) from Baturituba; Capricho do Ano (The Humor of the Year) from the district of Axixá; and Mensageiro (The Messenger) from Caratatiua. Third place went to the Bumba-meu-Boi troupe "Tirirical no. 3" from Cipriano Costa; Deus Padrinho (God's Godfather) of Vila Passos; and Novo Capricho (The New Humor) from Cavaco.

There were no more parade contests organized for Bumba-meu-Boi in Maranhão after 1965. However, articles in local newspapers and journals continued to document the public opinion of the Boi and the negative opinion expressed by the authorities. From these articles, a shift in public consensus from mere tolerance to total acceptance is evident. Bumba-meu-Boi became for the Maranhense an expression of pride. This feeling is voiced by Haroldo Moura who boasts that the organization and beauty of Bumba-meu-Boi in Maranhão is superior to that encountered in the entire northeast of Brazil. In 1977, Bumba-meu-Boi received its first recognition in academic circles with Regina de Paula Santos Prado's master's thesis "Todo Ano Tem: As Festas na Estrutura Social Camponesa" submitted at the Universidade Federal do Rio de Janeiro.

In short, Bumba-meu-Boi came to be accepted by the ruling class as the most representative expression of the Maranhense culture. This recognition is corroborated by the selection of Bumba-meu-Boi to represent the state at the interuniversity sport competitions in Brasília. It is recorded: "At the IXth Brazilian School Games, Maranhão won a gold medal not through its athletes, but through its artists. Maranhense folklore, represented by Bumba-meu-Boi with the style of the island of São Luis, was considered the most original."[16] Continuing his commentary on the Boi at the games, the reporter reproduces a section of a column from *O Bicho* expressing admiration of Bumba-meu-Boi from Maranhão. In conclusion the writer proudly elevates Bumba-meu-Boi to the national level:

> *The folklore of Maranhão, which was one of the most requested presentations here at the IXth Jogos Estudanties Brasileiro [Ninth Brazilian Scholastic Games] gave an excellent show when it was presented at the tower. The popular gathering place became even more crowded with those who wanted to see the Bumba-meu-Boi of matraca. Everyone, regardless of where they came from, joined in the contagious sound and dance of the young folklorists... This folklore wonder which definitively affirmed itself at the Jogos Es-*

tudanties Brasileiros *should be included on Brazil's calling card to the world.*[17]

The creation of the Federation for the Defense of Folklore Groups in Maranhão was a validation of its acceptance by the authorities and its ascension in the state's cultural life. In time, Bumba-meu-Boi became one of the major tourist attractions in Maranhão. To some, this rapid elevation of the Boi hindered the recognition of other cultural manifestations that coexisted with the Boi through the years. Virgílio Pinto laments this phenomenon:

> *In the vast cultural tradition of Maranhão, Bumba-meu-Boi has without doubt gained high diffusion and recognition. Perhaps it is because this manifestation has its strongest expression in this state. It is such that when one arrives in Maranhão, regardless of the month, he goes straight to ask where he could see the Boi. If this exaltation of the Boi emphasizes the traditional folkloric manifestation of Maranhão to the point of identifying it with Maranhão, giving reason to people to come and see it, on the other side, it detracts from other popular manifestations existing herein.... Tambor de Crioula also draws people, but without a doubt, it does not attract the majority of the population. Then, it is necessary that the Maranhense turn his attention to other manifestations. Better yet, they should stimulate them. Thus, the folklore of our land would be deeply rooted, and Bumba-meu-Boi, in spite of the frequent presentation, would not run the risk of losing the authenticity, as appears to have happened to many [traditions like it].*[18]

CONCLUSION

Bumba-meu-Boi had undergone many changes, both conceptual and stylistic, that have eased its assimilation and continuity in Maranhão. Even in spite of existing regional variations, certain basic features of Bumba-meu-Boi maintain their original forms. Among others, the satirical nature of the Boi continues to remind its participants and observers of the shameful past out of which the plot was conceived. This satirical nature, however, represents only one of the Boi's functions for its observers. Other functions include the use of Bumba-meu-Boi as a mechanism for social control and occasion for devotion and the renewal of personal covenants with adopted saints. The latter functions are best expressed in refrains and verses sung during the presentation of the Boi. The analysis of these song texts reveals what Merriam has referred to as the "ethos" of the culture, which helps to comprehend those people behind the expression and their society. Merriam writes, "Through the study of song texts it may well be possible to strike quickly through protective mechanisms to arrive at an understanding of the 'ethos' of the culture and to gain some perspective of psychological problems and processes peculiar to it."[19] Song lyrics are written metaphorical language that contains deep meanings envisioned by their authors. An understanding of song creators' mind reveals the reasons for which Bumba-meu-Boi was created by enslaved Africans.

CHAPTER V

Anatomy of Bumba-meu-Boi Song Texts

The analysis of Bumba-meu-Boi song texts raises two pertinent questions whose answers can only be derived from dissection of its constituent features: structure and content. In the present study, attention is given to the poetic structure of song texts to reveal their characteristic criteria and to the discussion of their content to bring forth hidden cultural values and their composers' reflected worldview and life experiences.

POETIC STRUCTURE

In both melody and lyrics, Bumba-meu-Boi songs result from a cooperative effort to improvise on prescribed and non-prescribed topics, as discussed in Chapter II. In their improvisations, individual attention is focused on poetic structure and on thematic unity of the verses' material. From the poetic standpoint, all text improvisations are developed in accordance with a set of poetic guidelines that determine physical structure, such as the number of lines in a verse and the rhyming practice.

Looking only at the first of these guidelines, two features become apparent. First, the basic unit in a verse is comprised of two-line couplets. This structure follows the style of *literatura de cordel* (popular poems and songs) practiced in northeast Brazil by the *repentistas*, poets who improvise verses spontaneously. The total number of lines ranges between four and ten, divided in two segments, each of which plays a specific role in the overall structure of the song. The first section, labeled (A) in the example below, contains the statement of the message to be conveyed by the singer. This statement is usually developed or commented upon in the second segment, labeled (B). Although the content of the first section changes with each singer, who may elaborate upon an aspect of the theme announced in the same segment by the first singer, that of the second segment usually is repeated by every singer at the end of his verse. The utilization of segment (B) in this manner allows it to become a unifying device between sometimes-diverse thoughts expressed by individual singers. Equally pertinent, segment (B) serves also as a cadence formula which indicates the end of the verse and as a refrain within each verse.

REFRAIN:

(A) *On the small ranch there is an ox*

Oh! It is a beauty

(B) *Oh! José Vale, oh! Irene's José*

Antenor has a captivating boa

VERSE:

(A) *They caught me and tied me up*

And they cut my hair

The rumor of my reputation

Oh! It is already in Rio de Janeiro

(B) *Oh! José Vale, oh! Irene's José*

Antenor has a captivating boa

(A) *Singing this song*

I remember my brother

Who is below the ground

(B) *Oh! José Vale, oh! Irene's José*

Antenor has a captivating boa

Closer examination of segment (B) in this song and in the other sixteen songs in which the practice is observed indicates that musically, segment (B) serves as a common denominator between the verses and the refrain, and as cadence formulae indicating that the singer has come to the end of his verse.

The second set of poetic guidelines requires rhyming of lines in all verses. A verse is referred to as being of *pé quebrado* (broken foot) when it lacks rhymes of any kind. According to José Vale, a performance of this kind of *toada* can be stopped by the master for failing to comply with these unwritten rules. "In fact," adds Mr. Vale, "only drunks intone songs with broken foot. To avoid offending the improvisers, I let them to go on with what they have started. Of course when it is really bad, nobody wants to sing it, anyway."[1] Within these ground rules there are several variations that attenuate their rigidity and open dimensions of tolerance to allow certain types of verses to be sung in spite of the state of their rhymes. In order to illustrate the rhyming practices in these songs I have left the texts in their original language. Their translations can be found in the translation section of this work.

The proper rhyming practice for *toadas* and verses is that in which lines rhyme according to both the phonetics and the spelling of the last syllables:

Oh! meu Senhor São João

Oh! me dê vida e saúde

Ative a minha memoria, São João

E meu cantar não se mude

Se eu morrer cantando boi, São João

Me cubra com sua virtude

[*Eu Já Rezei*]

The percentage of this type of verse with perfect rhyming is very low in an event where participants consume a large quantity of alcohol. In some troupes the responsibility of leading songs (i.e., improvising verses) is left to a selected few designated according to criteria such as strong leading voice and the ability to improvise rhyming verses on a wide variety of subjects. In the Boi de Zé Vale troupe, as in any other troupe in which all participants are given the opportunity to improvise verses, guidelines are modified to accommodate verses with a variety of rhyming patterns. These variations range from verses with two to three line rhyme with no specific order:

(A) *Toquei no meu apito*

Pra reunir meus companheiros

Oh! boi, oh! boi, boi!

Agora eu vou buscar meu galheiro

[*Agora eu vou Buscar meu Galheiro*]

(B) *Guarnece, guarnece*

Guarnece rapaziada

Cantou vaquelro bonito

Não guarnece boi nem nada

[*Guarnece*]

(C) *Esta turma é firmada*

Ela anda tangindo galheiro

Zé, Zé Vale, oh! companeiro

Agora em '82 nós vamos no Rio de Janeiro

[*Jiboia Atraidora*]

Further modifications are brought to these poetic guidelines. In this variation of the guideline, the rhyming is based only on phonetics rather than on the combination of phonetics and spelling. Word endings are given importance and often modified to rhyme with each other. Frequently the last syllables of words ending with *–or* are modified phonetically to rhyme with words ending with *–ou*, and the last syllables of words ending with *–ar* and *–al* are also modified phonetically to rhyme with those ending with *–a*.

(A) *Levante galheiro*

Te alevanta pra brincar

Seu Antenor

Que te batizou

[*Te Alevante Boi*]

(B) *Está chegando a hora*

De quem quer rezar

Mas, te ajoelha boi

Faz teu pelo sinal!

[*Está Chegando a Hora de Quem Quer Rezar*]

An interesting rhyming practice is encountered in "A Moça me Procurou" where the *–il* of Brazil is shortened in pronunciation to rhyme with *aqui* and Kazadi.

A moça me procurou

Quem cantou aqui?

o Zé Vale, governador do Brasil

Ele está elogiando professor Kazadi

[*A Moça me Procurou*]

In light of all these guidelines and variations devised to create a smooth flow of the presentation, many verses that would be considered to have broken foot constitute the corpus of tolerable rhyming practices. Their performance should be considered an exception and accidental. In the fifty songs included in this study, totaling one hundred and sixty verses, only two fall into this category.

(A) *Oh! boi, fala pro boi!*

Oh! boi eu vou levar o meu galheiro

Cantador de vaca de São João

Pra pagar sua promessa

[*Guarnece of Boi*]

(B) *Gente me fazem um silêncio*

Eu ouvi meu Amo chamar

Não sei se é pra meu bem

Não sei se é pra meu mau

[*Gente me Fazem um Silêncio*]

CONTENT

The second chapter discussed the presentation of the five-section Bumba-meu-Boi by the Boi de Zé Vale troupe in Pindaré, only two of which are structured. Their subject matter remains the same each year. The first of these, *Guarnição*, culminates in the presentation of the ox to the patron saint for sanctification and the renewal of personal covenants with Saint John, Saint Peter, and Saint Mark. As a result, the overall atmosphere maintained during this entire section is devotional. The second section with fixed subject matter is the *Matança*, in which the actual legend is dramatized. While these sections portray a prescribed subject matter, the other three sections, *Cordões*, draw their subject matter from the community. It is in these three sections that the cultural peculiarities of the troupe, which can be likened to a small community, are expressed. These differences stem basically from the community and especially the participants' occupations. If one is to understand this dimension of the social function fulfilled by Bumba-meu-Boi in their respective locales, one must focus on the content of the verses improvised during the sections in which singers are given license to express matters of personal concern.

In the *Cordão*, the diversity of subject matter included in the verses ranges from the personal to the communal. For many participants, Bumba-meu-Boi conjures up many memories. In the following verse, the singer remembers his brother who has passed away as he participates in Bumba-meu-Boi:

Singing this song

I remember my brother

Who is under ground

Oh! José Vale, oh! Irene's José

Antenor has a captivating boa!

[*A Captivating Boa*]

A similar expression of personal memory is encountered in another song:

When the month of June arrives

That I participate-in Bumba-meu-Boi

Even my heart hurts

Oh! Ox, ox, ox

But today you reminded me

Of a brother of mine

[*When the Month of June Arrives*]

Bumba-meu-Boi also offers to many the opportunity to boast about their personal strength and achievements in public. In "A Captivating Boa," there is a verse in which the singer sings about his fame, which has reached Rio de Janeiro. What is important in this verse is twofold: first there is the personal fame, the reputation that the singer wants to make public; second, Rio de Janeiro is the city dreamed about by members of the Pindaré community. Six other verses included in this study make reference to Rio de Janeiro always as the most envied place. Therefore, by boasting that his reputation has spread to Rio de Janeiro, the singer associates himself with the best. In the following example the singer praises his own strength and dares the wildcat:

> *Tomorrow I am going there*
>
> *I'll be going breaking barricades*
>
> *You are a mountain wildcat, and I am a man*
>
> *I want to see you eat me.*
>
> [*Bewitched Wildcat*]

Love for a person of the opposite sex is expressed in a subtle manner such as in "The Foot of a Rosebush."

> *I was at the foot of a rosebush*
>
> *The mist fell and soaked me*
>
> *Oh! Come here brunette*
>
> *I am your lover*
>
> *Come back home that the night is cold, and*
>
> *I want your warmth*
>
> [*The Foot of a Rosebush*]

Several songs can be classified as containing commentaries of on-the-spot situations such as boasting about the beauty of the event, praising one's troupe and the members' enthusiasm in the performance, and whatever else may have caught the singer's attention:

> (A) *This troupe is established*
>
> *It goes around performing Bumba-meu-Boi*
>
> *José, José Vale, oh! my companion*
>
> *Now in 1982 we will go to Rio de Janeiro*

[*A Captivating Boa*]

(B) *José Vale has an ox [has organized a Boi]*

When it bellows, it makes the ground tremble

It was born there on the small ranch

There are many [people] who would like to see it

Everybody wants to buy it

But, he [José Vale] does not want to sell.

[José Vale has an Ox]

or,

(C) *José Vale's troupe*

Oh! Jesus Christ has blessed it

It is a strong established group

Which does not mistreat singers

If you want to see what cattle rustle's roar is

Go to Antenor's small ranch

[José Vale's Troupe]

These are a few examples of improvisations praising the troupe and the beauty of its presentation. During one of the performances, participants would fight over the only microphone I had for a chance to be recorded. After several unsuccessful attempts to get to the microphone, a participant improvised this verse, which he addressed to those who were breaking the circle to sing ahead of him:

Singer, you are singing

Goodbye colleagues, together allow me

I came into this room

CHAPTER V

Goodbye brunette, to sing, allow me

You sang ahead of me

You made such a joke

You are mistaken

Give me permission [excuse me]

[I Went Out to Sing Bumba-meu-Boi]

Other incidences such as my presence and my smoking a pipe while recording were also subjects for verses:

(A) *A young lady asked me*

Who sang here?

José Vale, the Governor of Brazil

He is praising Professor Kazadi

[A Young Lady Asked Me]

(B) *Oh! Beautiful cattle drive*

Oh! Let me drive longhorn

Pal, you are smoking a pipe

But you don't offer it to your companion

[I Sent a Letter]

The performance of the Bumba-meu-Boi offers an opportunity for getting together and at the same time sets the stage for passing along hearsay. In the past, fighting among members of the same troupe was frequent primarily because of personal secrets or rumors being sung in a verse during the presentation.

Ah! Eh! Girl, ah! Eh! Beautiful girl

In the 1980 carnival you lost your honor

You didn't think well [straight]

Why didn't you do so

In 1981 you ran away and didn't get married

[Beautiful Girl]

The content of the *Cordão* section varies from one troupe to another, according to the occupations of the participants. In the Boi de Zé Vale troupe where there is a mixture of *vaqueiros*, fishermen, and farmers, the improvised song texts are heavily influenced by jargon from these occupations. One can guess with accuracy the occupation of a singer by the topic of his verse or by the vocabulary utilized in it. The following song text, for example, could only been improvised by a farmer:

Oh! When I die, I'll leave longing

To diverse companions

I have plenty of grain

Nobody pays attention to longhorn

Only I was born to sing

To the patron Saint John

[When I Die]

Fishermen songs speak of their occupational milieu and situations:

There is a star in the sky that illuminates the ocean

I heard a mermaid sing

She was on to a mound of rocks

She wanted to memorize my Bumba-meu-Boi songs

[I Heard a Mermaid Sing]

(B) *Midnight has struck*

The mermaid has sung

Come outside ox, Saint John has ordered

The tide has already changed

[Midnight has Struck]

(c) *On the Island of Mocoroca*

There is a bewitched wildcat

Which is eating fishermen

That is what I hear being said

[The Island of Mocoroca]

Several verses attest to the presence of *vaqueiros* in the Boi de Zé Vale troupe to be included as examples. However the following corroborate this assertion:

(A) *Benedito is good with the herd of cattle*

[But] José Vale is the driver of longhorn

Eh! Irene's José, Raimo

Marcela allowed cattle to be driven first

[Benedito is Good with the Herd of Cattle]

(B) *Oh! Enough, enough José Vale, this running bull*

Mané Motta has already tied up the gelding

I entered cattle rustling

I called my dog and put him on it

I am going to show to Benedito

How to strike the longhorn down

[Cattle Rustling]

Bumba-meu-Boi singers utilize some words that carry meanings of cultural value. To understand what the singer seeks to achieve with a particular utterance, it is necessary to be familiar with the social categories he uses and the cultural associations they carry for him. For example, in the song texts under consideration, there are several references to the word *sendeiro* (gelding). The explanation for this frequent reference is found in what the gelding means to the *vaqueiro* in Maranhão. Here, it is considered the *vaqueiro*'s best companion and a true worker. It is always ready and does not run after mares in heat. "This is a horse a man can depend on," explained one singer. "It is very expensive and a person who gives you a *sendeiro* is your true friend."

(A) *I have learned of the news*

That from Pindaré to the countryside

There is a ranch

On which an ox is attacking cowboys

Oh! José Vale

I bought my gelding

A magalaga horse

Which cost a hundred million cruzeiros

[Magalaga Horse]

(B) *Saint John is a rancher saint*

I am going to work on his ranch

It is now seven years that I was not

Speaking to him but we are talking this year

He gave me a gelding

[A Rancher Saint]

People in Pindaré have only a vague notion of the world outside of

CHAPTER V

their immediate community. They rarely visit the capitol of their state, and when the troupe has an engagement to perform in São Luis, it is an honor and a privilege to visit the city. Souvenirs from São Luis are cherished for a lifetime. However, whenever they want to make a reference to a foreign country, Rio de Janeiro and Portugal are mentioned. To some, even though I had said which country I came from, they still thought of me as coming from Portugal.

This troupe is established

It goes around singing Bumba-meu-Boi

José, José Vale, oh! Companion

Now in 1982 we will go to Rio de Janeiro

[A Captivating Boa]

Oh! ox, the cattle animates

Making the ground to tremble

I sing a modern song into the tape recorder

To take to Rio de Janeiro

[While I was Passing By]

Oh! ox, Bumba-meu-Boi performance

And Black man take a souvenir back with you

But you came here in Brazil

But you came to sight see

Take a souvenir of the longhorn

Oh! Black man, back with you to Portugal

[Turned Over Wood Ox]

CONCLUSION

In sum, the composition and the nature of Bumba-meu-Boi songs follow the *desafio* (verbal challenge) tradition established by the Portuguese in the northern Brazil during the colonial period. This tradition was based primarily on improvisation of both texts and their melodic counterpart to outdo one's opponent with the choice of words, rhymes, rhythm, and melody. Although the practice of the *desafio* is reserved today for special events, its impact is still prominent in the poetic structure of the *literatura de cordel*, popular songs of the *sertão* (remote hinterland), and Bumba-meu-Boi. In the earlier form of Bumba-meu-Boi, for example, *desafio* were a prominent part of the celebration. Today, Bumba-meu-Boi continues to obey the poetic guidelines that help structure verses with couplets as basic units.

The text of Bumba-meu-Boi songs is no longer competitive or aggressive, but elevating and devotional. It is not all comedy and satire, but also serious and thought provoking. It is not just communal, but also personal and very individual. The singer sets to music his praises and prayers to his adopted saint, and concerns from his daily life. He sings about his society and its lifestyle, sings about his physical and spiritual heroes, and sings about the wider world, which he has heard about but never seen. He unveils poetically and melodically the ill-behaved members of the community. All this functional content is presented in structured patterns according to a tradition of popular poetry.

CONCLUSION

This argument has made the following clear: As conceptualized and celebrated in Brazil, Bumba-meu-Boi is a folk drama containing dialogue, music, and dance depicting the interaction between the social classes in colonial Brazil. It is of neither individual nor learned authorship, but a product of communal effort. It served as a collective statement of retaliation by the oppressed against their oppressors, and as means by which the lower class denounced slave owners and ridiculed the ruling class. As such, Africans created Bumba-meu-Boi in Brazil during the Leather Civilization period (ca. 1750–1840). The tension between master and slave is characterized in the drama by the alliance of two oppressed groups—slaves and indigenous persons—against Portuguese masters. The slaves and indigenous persons share responsibility for sparking tension fanned by the slave's pregnant wife, Mãe Catirina, and in the restoration of communal harmony with the resurrection of the master's ox by the indigenous medicine man.

The symbolic death and resurrection of the ox do not constitute the hidden purpose for which Bumba-meu-Boi was created by the African, but to denounce slave owners and to serve as a vehicle of retaliatory mockeries for members of the lower classes against their oppressors. As a defense mechanism that protected their identity and ensured their survival in a hostile milieu, enslaved Africans formulated Bumba-meu-Boi as a cultural manifestation. The argument for the Afro-Brazilian authorship of Bumba-meu-Boi is sustained not only by its *raison d'être*, but also by the evolution of different styles, beginning with the African style called Boi de Zabumba, the indigenous style called Boi de Matraca (1868), and the introduction of the European style known as Boi de Orquestra in 1958. Such variants as Boi de Viola, introduced on the island of São Luis in 1999, are yet another assertion of a creative expression by participants in the capital city of Maranhão. As a new genre of cultural expression created by students, bankers, and learned members of the city of Sao Luis in 1984, Bozinho de Barrica has a different storyline centered on the quest for the star by the small wooden barrel-framed ox. The body of music, dance, and costume of this manifestation is composed of selected folk songs and dances from Maranhão performed in a potpourri of *toadas* belonging to Bumba-meu-Boi styles from the state. As such, Boizinho de Barrica assumes a non-ethnic identity.

Bumba-meu-Boi is both sacred and profane, characteristics reflected in the dual nature of its objectives. While it allows its participants to exteriorize their aggression through the mocking and repudiation of social sanctions, it also provides them with an opportunity to express profound devotion to Saint John, Saint Peter, and Saint Mark. The presentation of Bumba-meu-Boi is a festive occasion for communal merrymaking that brings members of the community closer to one another. It is also a period of communal devotion during which participants believing in miracles come together to seek good fortune from their patron saints. This dual nature of Bumba-meu-Boi is also evident in the roles played by the unifying element in the drama. While the ox is the source of deep-seated mockery against the ruling class, it is also the object of devotion. It is adorned, sanctified through baptism, and then offered to Saint John to serve as a link of covenant between the saint and the participants.

During the course of conducting fieldwork, several questions were raised that remain unanswered. One of them concerns the incorporation of the pregnant Mãe Catirina as the instigator of tension around which the entire drama evolves. Her specific request for the tongue from the master's favorite bull—Boi Estrela—has generated discussions among my students in the "Music of Latin America: Brazil" seminar at Kent State University, who have speculated about various interpretations, some of which are worth summarizing here. One interpretation and the most common is that this request reflects the cravings of a pregnant woman. Students have also interpreted this specific request as a means of breaking the cycle of poverty and bringing an economic balance between the lower and upper classes. Still other students attach a different significance to the act, postulating that it represents Mãe Catirina's hope that by eating the ox's tongue she will succeed in transferring to her unborn child all the characteristics of the Boi Estrela, ensuring fame and fortune.

The second unanswered question deals with how Saint John came to be the patron saint of Bumba-meu-Boi, the figure to whom participants make their requests and promises. While scholars seek elsewhere for the answer, I believe it can be found within the Brazilian culture. To a Brazilian, an individual's godfather has more authority over that person than his or her biological parents. Therefore, as Jesus' godfather, Saint John can directly order his godson to perform miracles on behalf of his (Saint John's) believers. Hence, promises made to Saint John by the participants are taken seriously.

The last but not least question concerns the placement of the star on the bull's forehead as a decorative motif on the animal's hide. Regardless of what scholars would like us to believe, this is not the star of Bethlehem but a visual identification of the bull's name—Boi Estrela—as it is referred to in the drama. In summation, all these social commentaries are presented within the framework of a musical drama to attenuate their impact and to serve as an instrument of social control used to protect communal harmony.

APPENDIX 1

Jibóia Atraidora

Rapaz tu Prestas Atenção

APPENDIX 1

Guarnece

APPENDIX 1

São João 'stá Aqui Seu Boi

Eu Ja Rezei

APPENDIX 1

Eu Ouvi uma Sereia Cantar

Pé da Roseira

APPENDIX 1

Benedito ele é Bom de Boiada

APPENDIX 1

Chega Chega Vaqueirama

É hora Nosso Boi Já Vai Morrer

Chico Matas o Boi

Boi Já Morreu

APPENDIX 1

APPENDIX 1

Bailarino das Areias

Carlos Dafé
Antonio José

APPENDIX 1

APPENDIX 1

APPENDIX 1

Coração Da Beira Mar

Carlos Dafé
Paulinho Jr.

APPENDIX 2

Transcription and Translation of Song Texts

Lyrics of songs are transcribed in the order members of the "King of Union" troupe in Pindaré performed them during the actual performance. Literary translation is provided to assist the reader submerge into the world of Bumba-meu-Boi. They are reproduced without editing to highlight the authenticity of the population's poetic creativity process. Spoken dialogue carried out between specific characters during the dramatization of the "Killing of the Ox" is also reproduced at the end of the lyrics.

JIBÓIA ATRAIDORA

Toada:

No sítio tem um Boi
Oh! é uma beleza
Oh! Zé Vale, oh! Zé d'Irene
Antenor tem uma jibóia atraidora!

Verso:

Fala, Boi, rapaziada!
É bonito que eu quero ver.
É hoje que gado apanha
Até dia amanhecer
Oh! Zé Vale, oh! Zé d'Irene
Antenor tem uma jibóia atraidora!
Me pegaram, me amarraram
E me cortaram meu cabelo
A fama do meu caraz
Oh! já está no Rio de Janeiro

Oh! Zé Vale, oh! Zé d'Irene
Antenor tem uma jibóia àtraidora!
Eu canto esta toada
Me lembro do meu irmão
Qu' está de baixo de chão
Oh! Zé Vale, oh! Zé d'Irene
Antenor tem uma jibóia atraidora!

A CAPTIVATING BOA

Refrain:

On the small ranch there is an ox,
Oh! it is a beauty
Oh! José Vale, oh! Irene's José
Antenor has a captivating boa!

Verse:

Speak, ox, young men!

145

APPENDIX 2

It is so beautiful that I want to see
It is today that we celebrate
Until the morning comes
Oh! José Vale, oh! Irene's José
Antenor has a captivating boa!
They caught me, and tied me
And they cut my hair
The rumor of my reputation
Oh! it is already in Rio de Janeiro
Oh! José Vale, oh! Irene's José
Antenor has a captivating boa!
Singing this song
I remember my brother
Who is below the ground
Oh! José Vale, oh! Irene's José
Antenor has a captivating boa
Oh! Boi, o gado apanha
O meu coração me doeu
Meu boiar vai-se embora
Vai pro Rio de Janeiro
Quem me dera que eu pudesse
Ir com ele
Esta turma é firmada
Ela anda tangindo galheiro
Zé, Zé Vale, oh! companheiro
Agora em '82 nós vamos
No Rio de Janeiro
Quem dera que pudesse
Si eu gastava dinheiro
Mas eu ia lá fora
Passear nos estrangeiros
Eu queria conhecer Pelé
O rei de futebol Brasileiro

Mas ele não quer vender
Oh! ox, cattle animate
My heart pains
My Bumba-meu-oi is going away
Going to Rio de Janeiro
I wish I could
Go along
This troupe is established
It goes around driving longhorn
José, José Vale, oh! companion
Now in '82 we will go
To Rio de Janeiro
I wish I could
If I spent money
But, I would go out there
Sightseeing in foreign countries
I would like to meet Pelé
The king of the Brazilian soccer

ZÉ VALE TEM UM BOI

Toada:

Zé tem um Boi
Quando ele urra, faz a terra tremer
Ele nasceu lá no sítio
Tem mais que deseja ver
Todo mundo quer comprar

JOSE VALE HAS AN OX

Refrain:

José Vale has an ox
When it bellows, the earth trembles
It was born there on the small ranch
There are many who wish to see it
Everybody wants to buy it
But, he (José Vale) does not want to sell

Verso:

Fala, Boi, rapaziada!
Adeus morena bonita
Que eu quero ver
Botando terra no lombo
E deixa notícia correr
Em cima do pau em pé
Lá deixa amarrado, combater.
Oh! Boi, oh! boiada!
Cantador, meu boiar é uma beleza
Eu cantei no gravador

É pra levar lá pro Rio de Janeiro
Zé Vale tem uma turma
É uma turma firmada
Ele tange o galheiro
Oh! Boi! na cabeceira do gado.
Oh! Boi, boiada!
Dizer boiada do meu Sr São João
Tu quer ver o Boi bonito
Tu vai no Antenor
Que tem um touro "Rei da União"
Oh! Boi, vai levando o Boi
Oh! meu vaqueiro,
Deixa o galheiro apanhar
Apanha de boca da noite
Até o dia raiar

Verse:

Speak, ox, young men!
Goodbye beautiful brunette
That I want to see
Throwing dirt on the ox's coat
Let the news to circulate
To the standing pillar
There leave it tied, to fight.
Oh! ox, oh! the presentation of theBoi!
Singer, my Boi is a beauty
I sang in the tape recorder
To be taken to Rio de Janeiro
José Vale has a group
It is an established one
He drives the long horn
Oh! Ox! in front of the cattle
Oh! ox! Bumba-meu-Boi!
Say Boi of my Lord Saint John
You wish to see a beautiful Boi?
Go to Antenor's small ranch
There is a bull "King of Union"
Oh! ox! Go on leading the ox
Oh! my vaqueiro,
Let the longhorn animate
It animates from dusk
Until the day break (dawn)

DOU UMA PISA NO GALHEIRO

Toada:

Oh! Boi, Boi, Boi!
Este ano eu
Dou uma pisa no galheiro
Na Primeira Cruz,
Nnasceu um novilho
Que está escarreirando vaqueiros

Verso:

Fala, Boi, rapaziada!
Deixa o dia amanhecer
Coisa que eu acho bonita
É um cantador de galheiro
Na Primeira Cruz,
Nasceu um novilho
Que está escarreirando vaqueiros
Bonito, rapaziada!
Deixa a matraca bater
Numa cabeceira neutra
Deixa notfcia correr
Na Primeira Cruz,
Nasceu um novilho
Que está escarreirando vaqueiro

GOING TO BE IN BOI

Refrain:

Oh! ox, ox, ox!
This year
I'm participating in Bumba-meu-Boi
On Primeira Cruz ranch,
Was born a bullock
Which is scattering vaqueiros

Verse:

Speak, ox, young men!
Let the morning come
Thing that I find beautiful

Is a singer of Bumba-meu-Boi
On Primeira Cruz ranch,
Was born a bullock
Which is scattering vaqueiros
Beautiful, young men!
Let the matraca sound
On a neutral heading
Let the news circulate
On Primeira Cruz ranch,
Was born a bullock
Which is scattering vaqueiros

UM SANTO FAZENDEIRO

Toada:

São João, é um santo fazendeiro
Vou trabalhar na fazenda dele
Está fazendo sete anos
Qu'eu não falava com ele
Nós estamos conversando este ano
Ele me deu um sendeiro

Verso:

Todo ano, todo ano eu canto Boi
Oh! Morena,
Nunca eu ganhei dinheiro
O meu prazer é cantar pra São João
Ele me ajuda
Pra mim tanger boi no terreiro
Está fazendo sete anos
Qu'eu não falava com ele
Nós estamos conversando este ano
Ele me deu um sendeiro

ZÉ VALE FEZ UM BOI

Toada:

Zé Vale fez um boi
Que está levantando poeira
Zequinha diz apanha ele

Mas assim mesmo fez sozinho
Zezinho não pode vir
Ajudar ele

A RANCHER SAINT

Refrain:

Saint John is a rancher saint
I am going to work on his ranch
It is now seven years
That I was not speaking to him
We are speaking this year
He gave me a gelding

Verse:

Each year, each year I sing in Boi
Oh! Brunette,
Never have I made money
My pleasure is to sing to Saint John
He helps me
To drive cattle in the field
It is now seven years
That I was not speaking to him
We are speaking this year
He gave me a gelding

JOSÉ VALE ORGANIZED BOI

Refrain:

José Vale organized a
  Bumba-meu-Boi
Which is stirring up dust
Zequinha said to come and get him
Even so, he (José Vale) did it alone
Zezinho could not come
To assist him

Verse:

Fala, Boi! Fala meu gado!

Fala, oh! gado no terreiro
O cantor mandou marcar
Oh! que lindo teu pandeiro
Zequinha diz apanha ele
Mas assim mesmo fez sozinho
Zezinho não pode vir
Ajudar ele

TOQUEI NO MEU APITO

Toada:

Toquei no meu apito
Foi pra guarnecer
Oh! meu São João
Oh! venha nós benzer
Nós livrar dos inimigos
Daqueles que querem nós vencer

Verso:

Eu chamei meus vaqueiros
É pra fazer a guarnição
Vou levar a brincadeira
Do meu Senhor São João
Oh! meu São João
Oh! venha nós benzer
Nos livrar dos inimigos
Daqueles que querem nós vencer

Verse:

Speak, ox! Speak my cattle!
Speak, oh! cattle in the field
The singer ordered to point out
Oh! how beautiful is your tamourine
Zequinha said to come and get him
Even so, he did it alone
Zezinho could not come
To assist him

I BLEW MY WHISTLE

Refrain:

I blew my whistle
In order to gather
Oh! my Saint John
Oh! come to bestow a blessing on us
To deliver us from our enemies
From those who wish to conquer us

Verse:

I summoned my vaqueiros
To organize the gathering
I am going to take the merrymaking
Of my Lord Saint John
Oh! my Saint John
Oh! come to bestow a blessing on us
To deliver us from our enemies
From those who wish to conquer us
Toquei no meu apito
Foi pra guarnecer
Chamei a vaqueirada
Pra cumprir com seu dever
Oh! meu São João
Oh! venha nós benzer
Nós livrar dos imigos
Daqueles que querem nós vencer

TOQUEI PRA GUARNECER

Toada:

Toquei chamando
Foi pra guarnecer
Meu São João,
Venha nós benzer
Pra nós livrar dos inimigos
Daqueles que quizer nós vencer

Verso:

Toquei chamando
"Rei da União", vaqueiro!

Mas eu chamei a minha vaquejada
A minha guarnição
O leite de país Brasileiro
É tão bonito com esta guarnição
Chamei a vaquejada
Que é pra guarnecer meu galheiro
I blew my whistle
To gather up
I summoned a group of vaqueiros
For them to fulfill their duty
Oh! my Saint John
Oh! come to bestow a blessing on us
To deliver us from our enemies
From those who wish to conquer us

I WISHTLED TO GATHER UP

Refrain:

I whistled calling
It was to gather up
My Saint John,
Come to bless us
To deliver us from our enemies
From those who wish to conquer us

Verse:

I summoned
The "King of Union," vaqueiro!
But I summoned my vaqueiros
My gathering
The milk of Brazilian country
Is so beautiful as this gathering
I summoned the round-up of cattle
To gather my longhorn
Oh! meu São João
Eu vou guarnecer
Vou guarnecer seu luar
Agora vou levar ele
Entregar no altar
Pra sua promessa pagar

BUSCAR MEU GALHEIRO

Toada:

Toquei no meu apito
Pra reunir meus companheiros
Oh! Boi, oh! Boi, Boi!
Agora eu vou buscar meu galheiro

Verso:

Vamos companheiros
Que as horas já estão chegada
Vou buscar meu galheiro
Oh! Boi, para ir pra vaquejada
Boi bonito da fazenda
Oh! Boi, vou buscar minha boiada
Vamos companheiros
Que já está chegada a hora
Vou buscar o meu galheiro
Com Deus e Nossa Senhora
Oh! my Saint John
I am going to gather
I am going to gather your moonlight
Now I am going to take it
And leave it at the altar
To fulfill your promise

TO BRING MY LONGHORN

Refrain:

I blew my whistle
To gather my companions
Oh! ox, oh! ox, ox!
Now I am bringing my longhorn

Verse:

Let us go companions
The hour has arrived
I am going to bring my longhorn
Oh! ox, to go round up the cattle
Beautiful ox of the ranch
Oh! ox, I am going to bring my herd

APPENDIX 2

Let us go companions
The hour has arrived
I am going to bring my longhorn
With God and Our Lady
Vamos, vamos companheiros
Vamos buscar o galheiro
Eu chamei a vaqueirada
Oh! Boi, chamei Primeiro Vaqueiro
Buscar "Rei da União"
Oh! Boi, de São João padroeiro

GUARNECE

Toada:

Guarnece, guarnece,
Guarnece rapaziada
Cantou vaqueiro bonito
Não guarnece boi nem nada

Verso:

Eu chamei Primeiro Vaqueiro
Chamei Vaqueiro Real
Oh! vaqueiro fala pra Boi
Oh! deixa Boi se levantar
Que São João está esperando
Em cima do seu altar
Guarnece, meu bom vaqueiro
Eu já mandei guarnecer
Eu vou fazer a guarnição
Pra a dona da casa ver
Let us go, let us go companions
Let us go to bring the longhorn
I summoned the group of vaqueiros
Oh! ox, I summoned the First
    Vaqueiro
To bring the "King of Union"
Oh! ox, of the patron Saint John

GATHER UP

Refrain:

Gather up, gather up,
Gather up young men
A handsome vaqueiro sang
He doesn't round-up cattle anything

Verse:

I summoned the First Vaqueiro
I summoned the Royal Vaqueiro
Oh! vaqueiro talk to the ox
Oh! let the ox get up
That Saint John is waiting
On his altar
Gather up, my good vaqueiro
I have already said to gather up
I am going to do the gathering
For the lady of the house to see
Oh! cadê Primeiro Vaqueiro
Cadê Vaqueiros Reais
Oh! Padre, entre a guarnição
Pra meu Boi se levantar
Que São João está esperando
Em cima do seu altar

GUARNECE O BOI

Toada:

Guarnece o Boi, guarnece o Boi
Guarnece o Boi na casa do cidadão
Eu vou pagar uma promessa
Que me ajude meu São João

Verso:

Oh! Boi, fala pro boi!
Oh! Boi, vou levar o meu galheiro
Cantador de vaca de São João
Pra pagar sua promessa

APPENDIX 2

BOI D'AURORA

Toada:

Boi lavanta, Boi d'aurora
Com Deus e Nossa Senhora

Verso:

Oh! levanta "Rei da União"
Oh! levanta do frio chão
Oh! where is the First Vaqueiro
Where are the Royal Vaqueiros
Oh! Priest, join the gathering
For my ox to get up
That Saint John is waiting
On his altar

ROUND UP THE CATTLE

Refrain:

Roundup, roundup the cattle
Roundup at the citizen's home
I am going to pay a promise
For Saint John to help me

Verse:

Oh! Ox, speak to the ox!
Oh! ox, I am taking my longhorn
Singer of Saint John's cow
To fulfill your promise

THE MORNING OX

Refrain:

Arise ox, the morning ox
With God and Our Lady

Verse:

Oh! arise "King of Union"
Oh! arise from the cold ground

Eu quero lhe levar
Pro altar do São João
Pra pagar uma promessa
Cumprir minha obrigação

BOI D'AURORA

Toada:

Boi lavanta, Boi d'aurora
Com Deus e Nossa Senhora

Verso:

Oh! levanta "Rei da União"
Oh! levanta do frio chão
Eu quero lhe levar
Pro altar do São João
Pra pagar uma promessa
Cumprir minha obrigação
Paquerada na porta
O boizinho está chorando

A ESTRELA DE CALDA

Toada:

Sai pra fora Boi
Que as horas estão se passando
Eu quero mostrar pra este povo
A estrela de calda lá brilhando
I want to take you
To Saint John's altar
To keep a promise
Fulfill my obligation

THE MORNING OX

Refrain:

Arise ox, the morning ox
With God and Our Lady

Verse:

Oh! arise "King of Union"
Oh! arise from the cold ground
I want to take you
To Saint John's altar
To keep a promise
Fulfill my obligation
Admirer (lover) at the door
The little ox is crying

A TAILED STAR

Refrain:

Come outside ox
That hours are going by (passing)
I want to show to these people
A tailed star shining there

Verso:

Sai pra fora Boi
Sai pra fora pro terreiro
Oh! veja como é tão bonito
Tu falas Boi, meu vaqueiro!
Vou te levar no altar
De São João padroeiro

MAIS QUEM DESEJAM TE VER

Toada:

Sai pra fora, Boi
Tem mais quem desejam te ver
São João está te esperando no altar
Pra receber

Verso:

Sai pra fora, Boi
Sai pra fora por terreiro
Vou te levar no altar

Com São João padroeiro
Veja como é tão bonito
Junto com meus companheiros
Vou levar meu Boi
Oh! essa linda brincadeira
Veja como é tão bonito
Com a turma brasileira
Essa turma está formada
Pra cantar Boi ano inteiro

Verse:

Come outside ox
Get out into the grounds
Oh! see how beautiful it is
Say ox, my vaqueiro!
I am going to lead you to the altar
Of the patron Saint John

MANY WISH TO SEE YOU

Refrain:

Come outside ox
There are more who wish to see you
Saint John is waiting at the altar
To receive you

Verse:

Come outside ox
Come outside into the grounds
I am going to lead you to the altar
With the patron Saint John
See how beautiful it is
Together with my companion
I am going to lead my ox
Oh! this beautiful merrymaking
See how beautiful it is
With a Brazilian group
This group is established
To sing Boi the entire year

EU VOU LEVAR MEU BOI

Toada:

Eu vou levar meu Boi
Restratado na bandeira
São João vai bem na frente
Guiando nossa trincheira

LÁ VAI MEU BOI

Toada:

Lá vai meu Boi
Com uma rosa na madeira
São João está no altar
Pra receber

Verso:

Lá vai meu Boi
Essa linda brincadeira
Eu vou levar minha turma
Oh! Boi! Numa casa brasileira
Eu vou levar meu galheiro
Com minha tripulação
Ele vai acompanhado
Até no altar de São João

I AM LEADING MY OX

Refrain:

I am going to lead my ox
Pictured on a flag
Saint John is going right ahead
Guiding our path

THERE GOES MY OX

Refrain:

There goes my ox
With a rose in the horns
Saint John is at the altar
To receive (you)

Verse:

There goes my ox
This beautiful merrymaking
I am going to lead my group
Oh! ox! in a Brazilian house
I am going to lead my longhorn
With my troupe
It goes accompanied
Until Saint John's altar

QUEM QUER VER

Toada:

Lá vai, lá vai
Lá vai Boi pra quem quer ver
Eu vou levar "Rei da União"
Fazendo a terra tremer

Verso:

Oh! lá vai Boi, oh! lá vai Boi
Junto com a tripulação
O Santo está esperando
No altar de São João
Eu vou levar "Rei da União"
Oh! com São João padroeiro
E veja como é tão bonito
Na chegada do terreiro

ESTÁ AQUI SEU BOI

Toada:

São João está aqui seu boi
Eu vim lhe trazer
Vim pagar sua promessa
Eu vim cumprir com meu dever

APPENDIX 2

Verso:

São João está aqui sua jóia
Quem trouxe fui eu
Vim pagar sua premessa
Que o devoto prometeu

WHO WISH TO SEE

Refrain:

There goes, there goes,
There goes the Boi, who wish to see
I am leading the "King of Union"
Making the ground to tremble

Verse:

There goes, there goes the ox
Together with the troupe
The Saint is waiting
At Saint John's altar
I am leading the "King of Union"
With the patron Saint John
And see how beautiful it is
At the arrival into the compound

HERE IS YOUR OX

Refrain:

Saint John here is your ox
I brought it to you
I came to keep your promise
I came to fulfill my duty

Verse:

Saint John here is your jewelry (gem)
It is I who brought it
I came to pay your promise
That the devout promised
São João está aqui seu boi
Oh! meu padroeiro

Vim pagar essa promessa
Junto com meus companheiros
Oh! me dê vida e saúde
Pra cantar no mundo inteiro
São João está aqui teu boi
Juntinho do altar
Eu tinha essa promessa
A ela olhando eu vou cantar
Está dentro do meu peito

MEU VAQUEIRO

Toada:

Meu vaqueiro
Estava na igreja pra dobrar-o-sino
Pra o Senhor São João saber
Que eu cheguei com meu pessoal

QUEM QUER REZAR

Toada:

Está chegando a hora
De quem quer rezar
Mas, te ajoelha Boi
Faz teu pelo sinal
Saint John here is your ox
Oh! my patron (Saint)
I came to keep this promise
Together with my companions
Oh! give me life and health
That I may sing in the entire world
Saint John here is your ox
Near the altar
I had this promise
To her looking, I am going to sing
It is inside my chest

MY VAQUEIRO

Refrain:

My vaqueiro
I was in the church to ring the bell
To let Lord Saint John know
That I have arrived with my troupe

WHO WISH TO PRAY

Refrain:

It is about time
For those who wish to pray
But, get down on your knees ox
And cross yourself

Verso:

Te ajoelha Boi bonito
No altar de São João
Pra receber a promessa
Fazer tua obrigação
Depois da promessa paga
Alegrar meu coração
Te ajoelha Boi bonito
São João foi quem mandou
Te ajoelha no altar
Esperando o rezador
Que é pra pagar essa promessa
Que devoto chamou

JÁ SE REZOU

Toada:

São João já se rezei
Já se acabou de rezar
Quero que me dê licença
Pra meu Boi se alevantar

Verso:

Oh! meu São João
Oh! levanta se galheiro
Que é pra levar eu pra rua
Junto com meus companheiros
Pra nós brincar lá na rua
Junto com meus companheiros

Verse:

Genuflect beautiful ox
At Saint John's altar
In order to receive the promise
Fulfill your obligation (duty)
After the promise has been kept
It will rejoice my heart
Genuflect beautiful ox
It is Saint John who ordered
Genuflect at the altar
Waiting for the praying
It is to keep this promise
That devout made

HAS BEEN PRAYED TO

Refrain:

Saint John has been prayed to
The praying is over
I want that you grand me permission
For my ox to arise

Verse:

Oh! my Saint John
Oh! rise your longhorn
Who is to take me to the street
Together with my companions
For us to play there in the street
Together with my companions
São João eu já rezei
Junto com meus companheiros
Eu quero que me dê licença
De eu levar o Boi pro terreiro

Esta turma está formada
Fala pra Boi meu vaqueiro

EU JÁ REZEI

Toada:

Eu já rezei
Pra meu Senhor São João
Eu já me alevantei
Eu vou chamar
O meu vaqueiro atenção

Verso:

Boa noite São João
O meu santo verdadeiro
Que meu dê vida e saúde, São João
Pra mim com meus companheiros
Vou pagar esta promessa, São João
Neste salão brasileiro
Oh! meu Senhor São João
Oh! me dê vida e saúde, São João
Pra mim com meus companheiros
Vou pagar esta promessa, São João
Neste salão brasileiro
Saint John, I have already prayed
Together with my companion
I want that you grant me permission
To lead the ox into the grounds
This troupe is organized
Speak to the ox my vaqueiro

I HAVE PRAYED

Refrain:

I've already prayed
To my Lord Saint John
I've already arisen
I am going to call
My vaqueiro's attention

Verse:

Good night Saint John
My true saint
Give me life and health, Saint John
To me and to my companions
I am paying this promise, Saint John
In this Brazilian hall
Oh! my Lord St. John
Oh! grant me life and health St. John
To me and my companions
I am fulfilling this promise, St. John
In this Brazilian hall
Oh! meu Senhor São João
Oh! me dê vida e saúde
Ative a minha memoria, São João
E meu cantar não se mude
Se eu morrer cantando Boi, São João
Me cubra com sua virtude
Oh! meu Senhor São João
Eu quero ser seu vaqueiro
Quero que me dar licença
De levar o Boi por terreiro
Eu já me alevantei, eu vou chamar
O meu vaqueiro atenção

TE ALEVANTE BOI

Toada:

Te alevante Boi
São João quem te mandou
Depois da reza
Tu te batizou

Verso:

Levante galheiro
Te alevanta pra brincar
Seu Antenor
Quem te batizou
Oh! my Lord Saint John
Oh! give me life and health
Active my memory, Saint John

APPENDIX 2

That my singing does not change
If I should die singing Boi Saint John
Cover me with your virtues
Oh! my Lord Saint John
I want to be your vaqueiro
I ask that you give me permission
To lead my ox into the grounds
I've already gotten up, I am calling
My vaqueiro's attention

ARISE OX

Refrain:

Arise ox
Saint John is ordering you
After the prayer
You were baptized

Verso:

Arise longhorn
Arise to play
Mr. Antenor
Is the one who baptized you
Levante Boi
Levante do frio chão
É tão bonitta nossa guarnição
Pagando a promessa
No altar de São João

NA SANTA IGREJA

Toada:

Cheguei na santa igreja
Eu rezei pra meu santo
Ajoelhado na igreja
Eu vou entregar minha alma
Pra meu Jesus Cristo e pra São Pedro

Verso:

De joelho eu fui no céu

Nos pés de Nosso Senhor
Eu fui buscar meu São João
Para o nosso defensor
Vós me dê a salvação
E com o destino do povo
Cadê meu São João
Já rezei meu São João
Pra pagar meus dever
Vim pagar sua promessa
E cumprir com meu dever
Eu vim fazer minha obrigação
Com todo gosto e prazer
Arise ox
Arise from the cold ground
It's so beautiful our gathering
Paying the promise
At Saint John's altar

IN THE HOLY CHURCH

Refrain:

I've arrived in the holy church
And have prayed to my saint
Kneeling in the church
I am going to offer my soul
To my Jesus Christ and to St. Peter

Verso:

On my knees I went to heaven
To our Lord's feet
I went to summon my Saint John
To be our defender
Thou give me salvation
And that destined to the people
Where is my Saint John
I've already prayed to my Saint John
To fulfill my obligations
Came to keep my promise
And satisfy my obligation
I came to do my task
Happily and joyfully

JÁ DEU MEIA NOITE

Toada:

Já deu meia noite
A sereia cantou
Sai pra fora Boi
Que São João mandou
A maré já deu virador

Verso:

O Boi bonito
Sai pra fora pro terreiro
Ele é tão bonito
Com São João padroeiro
Oh! Boi, fala pra Boi meu vaqueiro
Vamos embora galheiro
Já cansei de mandar
Eu vou levar meu Boi
Pra uma promessa pagar
Que o dono da casa
Está cansado de esperar
O Boi bonito
Desta nossa brincadeira
Eu vou levar meu Boi
São João foi quem mandou
Oh! Boi, numa casa Brasileira

MIDNIGHT HAS STRUCK

Refrain:

Midnight has struck
The mermaid has sung
Come outside ox
Saint John has ordered
The tide has already changed

Verse:

The beautiful ox
Come out into the grounds
It is so beautiful
With the patron Saint John
Oh! ox, speak to the ox my vaqueiro
Let us go longhorn
I'm tired of ordering
I am going to take my Boi
To fulfill a promise
That the owner of the house
Is tired of waiting
The beautiful ox
Of our merrymaking
I am going to take my ox
Saint John is the one who ordered
Oh! ox, in a Brazilian house

BOI DA MADEIRA PRETA

Toada:

Oh! Boi, Boi, Boi
Oh! Boi da madeira preta
Sai pra fora pra brincar, meu Boi
A tua promessa está feita

Verso:

Vamos embora meu galheiro
Pro terreiro pra brincar
Vamos fazer o cordão, meu galheiro
Pra poeira levantar
Oh! Boi bonito
Fora brincar no terreiro
Te alevante, Boi bonito
Fora brincar no terreiro
Veja como é tão bonito, criança
Fala pra Boi, meu vaqueiro
Vou tanger essa boiada bonita
Na casa do Brasileiro
Oh! Boi quando apanha
Fazendo a terra tremer
Quando chega mês de Junho,
Na vaquejada
Eu vou selar meu sendeiro

BLACKWOOD OX

Refrain:

Oh! ox, ox, ox
Oh! ox made of blackwood
Get out to play, my ox
Your promise has already been made

Verse:

Let us go my longhorn
Into the grounds to play
Let us go to make the circle, my
  longhorn
For dust to arise
Oh! beautiful ox
Out, to play into the grounds
Arise, beautiful ox
Out to play into the grounds
See how beautiful it is, children
Speak to the ox, my vaqueiro
Going to participate in this prety Boi
In a Brazilian house
Oh! when Boi animates
Making the ground to tremble
When June arrives,
In cattle rustling
I'll saddle my gelding

ZÉ RAIMUNDO TE PREPARE

Toada:

Toquei no meu apito
O São João quem me mandou
Oh! Zé Raimundo te aprepare
Eu já vou

Verso:

Oh! Boi, meu vaqueiro
Oh! vamos levar meu galheiro
Eu vou levar meu Boi bonito

Pra brincar no seu terreiro
Senhora me dê licença
De brincar no seu terreiro
Vou levar nosso Boizinho
Oh! pra brincar no seu terreiro
Oh! Zé Raimundo te aprepare
Eu já vou

O CAMPEÃO CHEGOU

Toada:

Chegou, chegou
O campeão do mundo chegou
É esse, é esse
Que a voz anunciou

JOSÉ RAIMUNDO GET READY

Refrain:

I blew my whistle
Saint John is the one who said to
Oh! José Raimundo get ready
I am coming

Verse:

Oh! Boi, my vaqueiro
Oh! let us lead my longhorn
I am going to lead my beautiful ox
To play in your grounds
Lady, give my permission
To play in your grounds
I am going to bring our little ox
Oh! to play in your grounds
Oh! José Raimundo get ready
I am on my way

THE CHAMPION IS HERE

Refrain:

He is here, he is here
The champion of the world is here
It's this, it's this
That the voice has announced

Verso:

Oh! Boi, oh! boiada
Não vamos falar pro galheiro
Amor como é bonito
Pra eu tanger boi no terreiro
Fazer boiada bonita
Com batalhão brasileiro

TURMA DE ZÊ VALE

Toada:

A turma de Zé Vale
Oh! Jesus Cristo abençou
É uma turma firmada
Não maltrata cantador
Tu queres ver que é rugião de boiada
Vai no sítio de Antenor

Verso:

Oh! Boi, o gado apanha
E meu coração meu doeu
Quando chega mês de Junho
Eu vou selar meu sendeiro
Essa turma de Zé Vale
É uma turma batuqueira
Este ano ela está firmada
Pra tanger gado
Na copa do mundo inteiro
Pra me ir nessa vaquejada
Junto com meus companheiros

Verse:

Oh! ox, oh! Bumba-meu-Boi
We are not speaking to the ox
Love, how beautiful it is
To rustle the cattle in the fields
To make a beautiful Boi
With a Brazilian batalion

JOSÉ VALE'S TROUPE

Refrain:

José Vale's troupe
Oh! Jesus Christ has blessed it
It is a strong established group
Which does not mistreat singers
If you want to hear what the roar is
Go to Antenor's small farm

Verse:

Oh! ox! The cattle animate
And my heart pains me
When comes the month of June
I'm going to saddle my horse
This José Vale's troupe
Is a happy (playful) troupe
This year it is established
To present the ox
In the World Cup
To go in this cattle rustling
Together with my companions

SAI PRA CANTAR BOI

Toada:

Saí pra cantar Boi
Junto com meus companheiros
Vai esse perder quem não veio
Essa turma de Zé Vale
Só tem tangidor de galheiro
Diz, oh! Zè d'Irene

Tu não deixas essas onças me comer

Verso:

Oh! minha sina foi essa
Com essa eu vou cumprir
Vou morrer cantando Boi
Com São João vou subir
Essa turma de Zé Vale
É carga demais pra galheiro
Diz, oh! Zé d'Irene
Tu não deixas essas onças me comer
Boi bonito nem era este
Adeus criança, bonito era o cantador
Mais bonita é a dona dele
Adeus criança, a velha do governador
Essa turma de Zé d'Irene
Tu não deixas essas onças me comer

I WENT TO SING BOI

Refrain:

I went to sing Bumba-meu-Boi
With my friends
Will miss this he who didn't come
This José Vale's troupe
Has only longhorn rustlers
Say, oh! Irene's José
Don't let these wildcats eat me

Verse:

Oh! This way my destiny
With this I'll accomplish (fulfill)
I'll die singing Bumba-meu-Boi
With Saint John I'll rise
This José Vale's troupe
Is too much for the longhorn
Say, oh! Irene's José
Don't let these wildcats eat me
Beautiful ox such was this
Goodbye child, beautiful was the singer
More beautiful is its owner
Goodbye child, the governor's old lady
This José Vale's troupe
Don't let these wildcats eat me
Cantador, tu estás cantando
Adeus colegas,
Junto me dá uma licença
Eu cheguei neste salão
Adeus morena,
Ppra mim cantar, com licença
Tu cantou na minha frente
Tu faz uma graca dessa
Tu t'inganou,
Dá licença

QUANDO EU MORRER

Toada:

Oh! quando eu morrer,
Eu deixo a saudade
Pra diversos companheiros
Eu tenho muita sementes
Ninguém liga pro galheiro
Só eu que nasci pra cantar
Pra São João padroeiro

Verso:

Eu vou cantar, com prazer
Eu vou, eu vou cantar no rugião
Junto com meus companheiros
Diz aí que Seu Zé Souza
Diz aí que Seu Zé Souza, São João
Singer, you are singing,
Goodbye colleagues,
Together allow me
I arrived in this hall
Goodbye brunette,
To sing, excuse me
You sang ahead of me,
You made such a joke

You are mistaken
Excuse me

WHEN I DIE

Refrain:

Oh! when I die,
I'll leave longing
To diverses companions
I have plenty of seeds
Nobody pays attention to longhorn
Only I was born to sing
To the patron Saint John

Verse:

I'll sing, with pleasure
I'll, I'll sing in the roar
Together with my companions
Say there, that Mr. José Souza
Say there, that José Souza, St. John
Eu nasci pra tanger galheiro
Eu tenho muita sementes
Ninguém liga pro galheiro
Só eu que nasci pra cantar
Pra São Soão padroeiro

MOÇA BONITA

Toada:

Ah! eh! moça, eh! moça bonita
No carnaval de '80
Tu perdeu teu valor
Você não pensou bem
Pra que tu não pensou
No ano de '81 você fugiu
Não casou

Verso:

Ah! ah! boi, eh! boi rapaziada
Fala Boi, rapaziada,

É bonito que eu quero olhar
Botando terra no lombo
Adeus criança,
Cantando pra meu Sr. São Marçal
I was born to drive longhorn
I have plenty of seeds
Nobody pays attention to longhorn
Only I was born to sing
To the patron Saint John

BEAUTIFUL GIRL

Refrain:

Ah! eh! Girl, eh! beautiful girl
In the 1980 carnival
You lost your honor
You didn't think straight
Why didn't you think so
In 1981 you ran away
And didn't get married

Verse:

Ah! eh! ox, eh! ox, young men
Speak ox, young men, is beautiful
That I would like to see
Trowing dirt on its cloak
Goodbye child, singing Boi
To my Lord Saint Mark
Que São me mandou
Você não pensou bem
Pra que tu não pensou
No ano de '81 você fugiu
Não casou
Você não pensou bem
Pra que tu não pensou
No ano de '81 você fugiu
Não casou
Eh! Boi, eh! Boi, eh! Compadre
É hoje que gado apanha
Deixa matraca trabalhar
É hoje que eu canto alegre

Na boca do gravador
Deixa notícia rolar
Você não pensou bem
Pra que tu não pensou
No ano de '81 você fugiu
Não casou
Eh! Boi, eh! Bom vaqueiro
Tanger Boi, tanger boiada
O meu cavalo cansou
Eh! Boi, adeus criança
Eu só vou nessa boiada
That Saint John has ordered me
You didn't think well
Why didn't you think so
In 1981 you ran away
And didn't get married
You didn't think well
Why didn't you think so
In 1981 you ran away
And didn't get married
Eh! Ox, eh! Ox, eh! Pal
It's today that the Boi animates
Let matracas (woodblocks) work
It's today that I joyfully sing
Into the tape recorder
Let the news spread
You didn't think well
Why didn't you think so
In 1981 you ran away
And didn't get married
Eh! Ox, eh! Good vaqueiro
To drive cattle, to drive herd of cattle
My horse is tired
Eh! Ox, goodbye child
I only will go in this cattle drive

IA PASSANDO

Toada:

Ia passando
Uma moça me chamou
Procurou aonde eu ia
Vou atraz do cantador
Vou me tanger uma boiada
Que meu São João mandou

Verso:

Oh! Boi, o gado apanha
Fazendo a terra tremer
Eu mando canto moderno
Na boca do gravador
Pra levar pro Rio de Janeiro

BOI DA MADEIRA VIRADA

Toada:

Oh! Boi, Boi, Boi
Oh! Bo da madeira virada
Eh! Zé Vale não me convidou
Você não queria
Que eu viesse na sua boiada

Verso:

Oh! Boi, gado apanha
E crioulo leva lembraça pra lá
Mas tu veio lá no Brasil
Mas tu veio passear
Tu levas uma lembrança do galheiro

AS I WAS PASSING BY

Refrain:

As I was passing by
A young lady called me
Wanting to know where I was going
I'm going after singer
I'm going to organize a Boi
That my Saint John ordered

Verse:

Oh! ox, the cattle animates

Making the ground to tremble
I sing modern song
Into the tape recorder
To take to Rio de Janeiro

TURNED OVER WOOD OX

Refrain:

Oh! ox, ox, ox
Oh! ox made of turned over wood
Eh! José Vale didn't invite me
You didn't want me
To participate in your Boi

Verse:

Oh! ox, Bumba-meu-Boi animates
And Blackman take a souvenir back
But you came there in Brazil
But you came to visit
Take a souvenir of the longhorn

CAVALO MAGALAGA

Toada:

Eu sobe de notícia
Que do Pindaré pro sítio
Tem uma fazenda
Que o touro está dando em vaqueiros
Oh! Zé Vale,
Eu comprei meu sendeiro
Um cavalo magalaga
Que custou cem milhão de cruzeiros

Verso:

Fala Boi, rapaziada
Adeus criança, deixa notícia correr
Num cabeceira neutra
Adeus morena, deixa matraca bater
Eu estando cantando alegre
Adeus criança,

Pra São João padroeiro

EU 'VI UMA SEREIA CANTAR

Toada:

No céu tem uma estrela
Que alumeia o mar
Eu ouvi uma sereia cantar
Ela está em cima de monte de pedra
Ela quer é decorar meu boiar

MAGALAGA HORSE

Refrain:

I've learned of the news
That from Pindaré to the country side
There is a ranch
On which an ox is attacking vaqueiros
Oh! José Vale
I bought my gelding
A magalaga horse
Which cost a hundred million cruzeiros

Verse:

Speak ox, young men!
Goodbye child, spread the news
In a neutral position ahead of the herd
Goodbye brunette, let matraca sound
I'm singing joyfully
Goodbye child,
To the patron St. John

I HEARD A MERMAID SING

Refrain:

There is a star in the sky
That illuminates the ocean
I heard a mermaid sing
She was on top of a mound of rocks
She wanted to learn my Boi song

Verso:

Se eu morrer cantando Boi
Adeus criança e morena
Leva saudade e paixão
Eu vou mandar pra fazenda
Adeus criança, pra meu Sr. São João

ONÇA MONDONGUEIRA

Toada:

Na Ilha de Mocoroca
Tem uma onça mondongueira
Está comendo pescadores
É só que eu vejo dizer
Amanhã eu vou pra lá
Eu vou quebrando barreira
Tu és onça da montanha,
Eu também sou homem
Eu quero ver você me comer

Verso:

E lavaram o terreiro
Homem, lavaram o terreiro
Com vassoura de botão
Varridor meu Boi é branco
Não pode arrastar no chão
Amanhã eu vou pra lá
Eu vou quebrando barreira
Tu és onça da montanha,
Eu também sou homem
Eu quero ver você me comer

Verse:

If I should die singing Boi
Goodbye child and brunette
Take longing and passion
I am going to send it to the ranch
Goodbye child, to my Lord St. John

BEWITCHED WILDCAT

Refrain:

On the Island of Mocoroca
There is a bewitched wildcat
Which is eating fishermen
That is what I heard being said
Tomorrow I am going there
I'll be going breaking barricades
You are mountain wildcat,
And I am a man
I want to see you eat me

Verse:

And they swept the grounds
Man, they've swept the grounds
With a grass broom
Sweeper, my ox is white
It cannot be dragged on the ground
Tomorrow I am going there
I'll be going braking barricades
You are mountain wildcat,
And I am a man
I want to see you eat me

MÊS DE JUNHO

Toada:

Quando chega mês de Junho
Que eu canto a boiada
Até meu coração me doeu
Oh! boi, boi, boi!
Mas hoje tu fez me alembrar

Do mano me

A MOÇA ME PROCUROU

Toada:

A moça me procurou
Quem cantou aqui?
O Zé Vale, Governador do Brasil
Ele está elogiando Professor Kazadi

Verso:

O senhor, Seu Kazadi
Oh! eu sei tanger bem galheiro
Você está gravando minha toada
Bota no disco
E leve pros estrangeiros

THE MONTH OF JUNE

Refrain:

When arrives the month of June
That I participate in
  Bumba-meu-Boi
Even my heart hurts
Oh! ox, ox, ox!
But today you reminded me
Of a brother of mine

A YOUNG LADY ASKED ME

Refrain:

A young lady asked me
Who sang here?
José Vale, Governor of Brazil
He is praising Professor Kazadi

Verse:

Sir, Mr. Kazadi

Oh! I know to rustle longhorn
You are recording my song
Put it in disc
and take it to foreign countries

PRESTAS ATENÇÃO

Toada:

Rapaz tu prestas atenção
Que este touro quase mata
Teu sendeiro
Pega vara de ferrão
Enfiar no lombo dele
Saia boiando, pro gado, dizendo
Novilho respeita vaqueiro

PÉ DA ROSEIRA

Toada:

Eu estava no pé da roseira
Sereno caiu me molhou
Oh! vem cá morena
Eu sou teu amor
Volta pra casa que a noite está fria
E eu quero teu calor

Verso:

Oh! que boiada bonita
Está bom pra imperador
Olha a terra no lombo
Cantando pra tourador (rourada)
Quando eu estou na boiada,
Eu mando a toada
E o galheiro apanhou
Quando eu digo "lá vem Boi"

APPENDIX 2

PAY ATTENTION

Refrain:

Pay attention young man
That this bull has almost killed
Your gelding
Take a metal rod
Run it through his hide
Get mad at the cattle, saying
Bullock respect vaqueiro

THE FOOT OF A ROSEBUSH

Refrain:

I was at the foot of a rosebush
The mist fell and soaked me
Oh! come here brunette
I am your lover
Come home that the night is cold
And I want your warmth

Verse:

Oh! what a beautiful Boi
It is good for the emperor
Look at soil on the ox's cloak
Singing to the tourador (herd of bulls)
When I am in Boi,
I am leading a song
And the longhorn animated
When I say "there comes the ox"
Quem quiser
Que venha ver boiada bonita
Fazendo a terra tremer
Eu tanjo a vaquejada
É uma beleza
Boi apanha como quer

JAGADOR DO BRASIL

Toada:

O maior jagador do Brasil
Foi Pelé
Que jogou no mundo inteiro
Dizer, viva criança, essa brincadeira
Viva toda autoridade
De seleção brasileira

BATIDA DO GADO

Toada:

Oh! chega, chega Zé Vale,
Este touro, corredo
Mané Motta já cansou o sendeiro
Peguei batida do gado
Chamei meu cachorro e botei
Vou mostrar pra Benedito
Como é que se derriba galheiro
Those who wish,
Come and see the beautiful Boi
Making the ground to tremble
I rustle in the cattle round-up
It is a beauty
Animates like nothing

BRAZILIAN SOCCER PLAYER

Refrain:

Pele was
The best Brazilian soccer player
Who played all over the world
Say, viva child, this merrymaking
Hurrah! to all authorities of the
Brazilian soccer selection

APPENDIX 2

CATTLE RUSTLING

Refrain:

Oh! enough, enough José Vale,
This running bull
Mané Motta rested the horse
I entered cattle rustling
I called my dog and put him on it
I am going to show to Benedito
How to strike down the longhorn

Verso:

Oh! Boi, cantor
Vamos cantar pra meu Sr. S. João
Oh! Boi, meus colegas
Com minha matraca na mão
Peguei batida do gado
Chamei meu cachorro e botei
Vou mostrar pra Benedito
Como é que se derriba galheiro

BOM DE BOIADA

Toada:

Benedito, ele é bom de boiada
Zé Vale é tangedor de galheiro
Eh! Zé de Irene, Raimundo
Marcela deixou tanger gado primeiro

Verso:

Em casa quando apanha a criança
Apanha até amanhecer
Onde eu estou na boiada, criança
E eu canto alegre
De fazer a terra tremer
Eh! Zé de Irene, Raimundo
Marcela dexou tanger gado primeiro

Verse:

Oh! Ox, singer

Let us sing to my Lord Saint John
Oh! Ox, my colleagues
With my matraca in hand
I entered cattle rustling
I called my dog and put him on it
I am going to show to Benedito
How to strike down the longhorn

GOOD WITH THE CATTLE

Refrain:

Benedito is good with the Boi,
But José Vale drives longhorn
Eh! Irene's José, Raymond
Marcela allowed cattle first

Verse:

At home when the child animates
He animates until morning
When I am in Bumba-meu-Boi, child
And I joyfully sing
To make the ground tremble
Eh! Irene's José, Raymond
Marcela allowed cattle first

TOADA DE PRESENTE

Toada:

Vou tirar uma toada
Eu vou dar de presente por um gravador de primeira
Tu levas na Difusora
Que eu também sou Brasileiro
Tu levas pra zona franca
E pra aeroportos estrangeiros

Verso:

É assim que gado apanha,
dizia meu colega

APPENDIX 2

Gado apanha como quer
Mas eu vou tanger boiada
Na copa do mundo inteiro
Tu levas na Difusora
Que eu também sou Brasileiro
Tu levas pra zona franca
E pra aeroportos estrangeiros

MARIA CELESTE

Toada:

Oh! Maria, Maria Celeste
Eu só quero pra ti me dizer
Se a nossa amizade
Se acabou de uma vez
Tu pensavas que eu não vinha
E, tu nem apareceu
A boiada de '81

A GIFT OF SONG

Refrain:

I am composing a song
And give it as a gift to a
Quality tape recorder
Take it to Difusora
For I also am Brazilian
Take it to duty free port
And to foreign airports

Verse:

This is how the cattle animates,
Said my colleague
Cattle animate as they want
But I am going to drive the herd
In the world cup tournament
Take it to Difusora
For I also am Brazilian
Take it to duty free port
And to foreign airports

MARIA CELESTE

Refrain:

Oh! Maria, Maria Celeste
I only want you to tell me
If our friendship
Has totally ended
You thought that I wouldn't come
And, you didn't even show up
The 1981 Bumba-meu-Boi

Verso:

Vá Boi! Fala Boi! Rapaziada!
Fala Boi!
Rapaziada destes crianças
Deixa notícia correr
Na boca do gravador
Meus amigos, adeus crianças,
Adeus morena
Deixa notícia correr
Tu pensavas que eu não vinha
E, tu nem apareceu
A boiada de '81
Que fez eu me lembrar de você

CUIDADO COM SUA TURMA

Toada:

Lá no sítio tem um Boi
É só que eu vejo dizer
É Zé Vale quem vai fazer
Oh! meu São João
Tem cuidado com sua turma
Não deixa que ser nós vencer

Verse:

Go ox! Speak ox! Young men
Speak ox!
Young men of these children
Let the news spread

Into the microphone of the recorder
My friends, goodbye children,
  Goodbye brunette
Let the news circulate
You thought that I wouldn't come
And, you didn't even show up
The 1981 Bumba-meu-Boi
Made me think of you

PROTECT YOUR TROUPE

Refrain:

In the small farm there is an ox
That is all that I hear being said
It is José Vale who is the one
Oh! my Saint John
Take care of your troupe
Don't let who may be conquer us

Verso:

Oh! Boi, oh! Boi, fala criança
Deixa o galheiro apanhar
Oh! meu São João
Estou com a matraca na mão
Pra mim tanger Boi no vale
Oh! meu São João
Tanger, galheiro apanha
Até o dia raiar

TOME CONTA DO SEU GADO

Toada:

Oh! meu São João
Tome conta do seu gado
Seus empregados
Não querem mais me atender

Verso:

O que eu quero

Eles não querem,
Que eles querem
Não vou querer
Agora cada qual
vai ficar com seu saber

Verse:

Oh! oh! ox, speak child
Let the Bumba-meu-Boi animate
Oh! my Saint John
I am with the matraca in my hand
To drive cattle in the valley
Oh! my Saint John
In cattle driving longhorn animates
Until dawn

PROTECT YOUR CATTLE

Refrain:

Oh! my Saint John
Take care of your cattle
Your workers
Don't want to listen to me anymore
Verse:
What I want
They don't want,
What they want
I will not want
Now each one of us
Will keep his knowledge

ONDE TU VAI?

Toada:

Onde tu vai morena?
Eu vou ver uma boiada
No sítio da Primeira Cruz
E do São João padroeiro
Zé Vale que está mandando
Junto com seus companheiros

Em '81, ele está
Com uma turma firmada
Pra cantar no mundo inteiro

Verso:

Se eu morrer cantando Boi
São João faz meu entêrro
São Pedro, Marçal, Marçal
Concorrem com toda despesa
Zé Vale que está mandando
Junto com seus companheiros
Em '81 ele está
Com um turma firmada
Pra cantar no mundo inteiro

EU MANDEI UMA CARTA

Toada:

Eu mandei uma carta
Zé Vale não me respondeu
Eu não sei se ele não
Me queimar na boiada, ou se foi
Armando que se aborreceu

WHERE ARE YOU GOING?

Refrain:

Where are you going brunette?
I am going to see a Bumba-meu-Boi
On Primeira Cruz ranch
And the patron Saint John
It is José Vale who is leading
Together with his companions
In 1981, he has
An established troupe
To sing in the whole world

Verse:

If I should die singing Boi
Saint John do my burrial

Saint Peter, Mark, Mark
Cover all the expenses
It is José Vale who is leading
Together with his companions
In 1981, he has
An established troupe
To sing in the whole world

I SENT A LETTER

Refrain:

I sent a letter
José Vale did not answer me
I don't know if he does not
Hurt me during Boi, or was it
Armando who was annoyed

Verso:

Oh! Boi, tanger bonito
Oh! deixa eu tanger galheiro
Compadre, tu estás
Com cachimbo no queixo
Mas tu não dás pra teu companheiro

NOSSO BOI JÁ VAI MORRER

Toada:

É hora, é hora
Nosso Boi já vai morrer

Verso:

Aparece Primeiro Vaqueiro
Prepara pro meu Boi brincar
Fala pro Boi, bom vaqueiro
Ma porteira do curral
Fala pro Boi, bom vaqueiro
Não deixa meu Boi te dar
Fala Boi, meu vaqueiro
Traz o Boi de lá pra cá

Te retira meu vaqueiro
Procurando teu lugar
Oh! aparece of Segundo
Prepara pra meu Boi brincar

Verse:

Oh! ox! Beautiful cattle drive
Oh! let me drive longhorn
Pal, you have
A smoking pipe in your jaw
But you don't give to your friend.

OUR OX IS GOING TO DIE

Refrain:

The hour has come
For our ox to die

Verse:

Appear, the First Vaqueiro
Get ready for my ox to play
Speak to the ox my vaqueiro
At the gate of the corral
Speak to the ox my good vaqueiro
Don't let it hit you
Speak to the ox my vaqueiro
Bring it from there to here
Withdraw yourself my vaqueiro
Search for your place
Appear, the Second Vaqueiro
Get ready for my ox to play
Oh! fala pro Boi meu vaqueiro
Deixa o Boi te conhecer
Oh! este Boi tem de costume
Antes de apanhar, bater
Oh! que meu Boi é bicho brabo
Nunca aprendeu rezar
Tome cuidado com este Boi
Não deixa ele te furar
Oh! este Boi tem ponta acima
É capaz de te furar

Oh! traz o Boi de lá pra cá
Bonito que eu quero ver
Oh! meia lua o meu Amo
Procurando seu lugar
Oh! aparece o bom Caboclo
Prepara pra Boi luvar
Oh! meu Boi está no terreiro
Está na hora de morrer
Oh! aparecem Nego Chico,
Catirina, Cazumbas
Speak to the ox my vaqueiro
Let it get used to you
This ox has the habit
Before it is hit, it hits
My ox is a wild animal
It never learned to pray
Look out with this ox
Don't let it hurt you
Oh! this ox with upward horn
Is capable to hurt you
Bring the ox from there to here
The beautiful ox that I want to see
Half-moon my Master
Search for your place
Appear my good Caboclo
Get ready to praise the ox
My ox is into the grounds
It is time for it to die
Appear Black Chico,
Catirina, and Cazumbas
Oh! Nego Chico, fala o Boi
Trazendo de lá pra cá
Oh! Nego Chico traz o Boi
Pra curtina de curral

CHICO MATAS O BOI

Toada:

Chico matas o boi
Se tu quers matar

APPENDIX 2

Verso:

Com essa espingarda
Nego velho Cazumba
Carrega essa espingarda
Pra no meu boi vai atirar
Carrega essa espingarda
Sem fecho e sem guarda-mão
Paquerando "Boi Estrela"
Na noite de São João
Paquerando "Boi Estrela"
Pela noite de São João
Carrega, Chico carrega
Carrega, va carregar
Black Chico, speak to the ox
Bringing it from there to here
Black Chico bring the ox
By the gate of the corral

CHICO KILL THE OX

Refrain:

Chico kill the ox
If you are going to do it

Verse:

With this shotgun
Old black Cazumba
Carry this shotgun
Cause at my ox you will shoot
Carry this shotgun
Without lock or holster
Flirting with the "Star Ox"
On Saint John's Night
Flirting with the "Star Ox"
On Saint Peter's Night
Carry, Chico carry
Carry, go to carry
Paquerando "Boi Estrela"
Na noite de João Marçal
Carrega, Chico carrega
Lá vem o touro acolá

Ele vem quebramdo a bareora
E peoira levamtar
Lá vem o touro acolá
Ele vem quebrando a bareira
Carrega, Chico carrega
Prepare e atire ligeiro
Lá vem o touro acolá
Escarerando vaqueiros
Carrega, Chico carrega
Chico tu prestas atencão
Carrega essa espingarda
Sem fecho e sem guarda-mão
Bater lá no "Boi Estrela"
Na veia do coração
Bater lá no "Boi Estrela"
Com meu boi cair no chão
Flirting with the "Star Ox"
On Saint Mark's Night
Carry, Chico carry
There comes the bull
It is coming breaking barricades
And raising dust
There comes the bull
It is coming breaking barricades
Carry, Chico carry
Aim and shoot lightly
There comes the bull
Scattering cowpunchers
Carry, Chico carry
Chico pay attention
Carry this shotgun
Without lock or holster
Shoot there at the "Star Ox"
Until my ox falls to the ground
Shoot there at the "Star Ox"
At the heart's blood vessel
Carrega essa espingarda
E Chico vai carregar
Bater lá nosso boi
Quero ver nosso boi deitar
Vamos ver ele cair no chão
Pra poeira levantar
Atire, Chico atire

Cuidado não vai errar
Atire em cima da testa
Não deixe o touro voltar
Cuidado Nego Chico
Lá vem o touro acolá
Atire no "Boi Estrela"
É hora de atirar
Meu vaqueiro traz o boi
Pra Nego Chico atirar
Eh! Chico presta atenção
É a hora que eu mandar
Carry this shotgun
And Chico you will carry
Shoot there at our ox
I want to see our ox lay down
Let us see it fall to the ground
And dust to arise
Shoot, Chico shoot
Be careful don't miss
Shoot on the forehead
Don't let the bull return
Look out Black Chico
There comes the bull
Shoot at the "Star Ox"
It is time to shoot
My vaqueiro bring the ox
For Black Chico to shoot at
Eh! Chico pay attention
On my mark

CHEGA VAQUEIRAMA

Amo:

Chega, chega vaqueirama
Na noite de São João
Pra aguentar nosso boi,
Meu vaqueiro
Não deixa cair no chão

Chico:

Estava brincando com boi

Mas não queria matar
Arma foi quem desparou,
Meu Amo
Matou seu fama real
Estava brincando com boi
De baixo da verde rama
Arma foi quem desparous,
Meu amo
Matou o boi de fama
Estava brincando com boi
Na rua da Floresta
Arma foi quem desparou,
Meu Amo,
Abriu um rombo na testa

GATHER UP VAQUEIROS

Master:

Gather up, vaqueiros
On Saint John's Night
To mourn our ox,
My vaqueiro
Don't let it fall to the ground

Chico:

I was playing with the ox
But I didn't mean to kill it
The shotgun discharged itself,
My Master
And killed your "Royal Fame"
I was playing with the ox
Beneath the green branches
The shotgun discharged itself,
My Master
And kill the famed ox
I was playing with the ox
There on the hill
The shotgun discharged itself,
My Master
Opened a hole on its forehead
Eu mandei fazer um cano

APPENDIX 2

Da culatra de latão
Pra atirar neste boi, meu Amo
Na veia do coração
Eu mandei fazer um cano
Da culatra de três dedos
Pra atirar neste boi, meu Amo
Bem na maçã do peito
Eu mandei fazer um cano
Da culatra de metal
Pra atirar neste boi, meu Amo
Quero ver ele deitar
Eu estava brincando com boi
Lá em cima do outeiro
Arma foi quem desparou,
Meu Amo
Se foi cair de mim
Estava brincando com boi
Na rua do Macapá
Arma foi quem desparou, meu Amo
Abriu um rombo na pá

I requested a barrel to be made
Of the tin
In order to shoot this ox, my Master
At the heart's blood vessel
I requested a barrel to be made
Measuring three fingers in diameter
In order to shoot this ox, my Master
Right on the brisket
I requested a barrel to be made
Of iron
In order to shoot this ox, my Master
I want to see it lay on the ground
I was playing with the ox
There on the hill
The shotgun discharged itself,
My Master
While falling out of my hands
I was playing with the ox
On Macapa Street
The gun discharged itself, Master
And opened a hole in thie

Chico:

Estava brincando com boi
Lá em cima no tesouro
Arma foi quem desparou,
Meu Amo
Abriu um rombo no couro

Amo:

Grand espingarda malvada
Espingarda do Pai Francisco
Aonde bateu um caroço,
Meu vaqueiro
É mesmo que esse é um corisco

Chico:

É um, é um corisco
Quando dá no pequizeiro
Queima capim-acu, meu Amo
Que dira lã de carneiro

Amo:

Tu queima lã de carneiros
Destes que nasceram agora
Mas do meu boi
Tu não queima Francisco
É joia de Nossa Senhora

Chico:

I was playing with the ox
There on top of the wealth
The shotgun discharged itself,
My Master
And opened a hole in the hide

Master:

The cursed big shotgun
Father Francisco's shotgun
Where it shot the bullet,
My vaqueiro
It looks like a lightning

APPENDIX 2

Chico:

> Yes, it is a lightning
> When it hits a tree
> It burns a bluestem, my Master
> What would say, lamd wool

Master:

> You can burn wool from lambs
> Of these new born
> But that of my ox
> You will not burn Francisco
> It is a jewel of Our Lady
> Chega, chega vaqueirama
> Na noite de São João
> Pra aguentar nosso boi,
> Meu vaqueiro
> Não deixa cair no chão
> Chega, chega vaqueirama
> Pela noite de São Pedro
> Pra aguentar nosso boi,
> Meu vaqueiro
> Nã deixa cair de medo
> Cadê minha toalha nova
> Dessas que chegaram agora
> Pra botar o boi do teu Amo, vaqueiro
> Com Deus e Nossa Senhora

BOI JÁ MORREU

Vaqueiro:

> Boi já morreu, já morreu

Toada

> Já morreu fama real
> Já morreu boi do meu Amo
> Deixa penna pra chorar
> Gather up, cowpunchers
> On Saint John's Night
> To mourn our ox,
> My vaqueiros
> Don't drop it

> Gather up, cowpunchers
> On Saint Peter's Night
> To mourn our ox,
> My vaqueiros
> Don't drop it of fear
> Where are my new towels
> Of those which just arrived
> To hold your Master's ox, vaqueiros
> With God and Our Lady

THE OX HAS DIED

Vaqueiro:

> The ox has died

Refrain

> The Royal Fame has died
> My Master's ox has died
> And leaves sadness for crying

Verso:

> Cadê meu chapéu de couro
> Minha vara de ferão
> Pra mim ir na vaqueijada
> Na noite de São João
> Minha vara de ferão
> Meu chapéu de alvoredo
> Pra mim ir na vaqueijada
> Numa noite de São Pedro
> Meu chapéu de alvoredo
> Minha corda de laçar
> Pra mim ir na vaqueijada
> Na noite de São Marçal
> Oh! grande penna eu teve hoje
> Grande penna eu teve agora
> De ver o nosso boi morto
> Na porta dessa senhora
> Sendo eu pobre vaqueiro
> Que andou na capoeira
> Encontrei o nosso boi
> Ele morreu de bicheira

APPENDIX 2

Sendo eu pobre vaqueiro
Que ando campeiando
Eu saí segunda feira
Cheguei no meio da semana

Verse:

Where is my leather hat
My iron rod
For me to go cowpunching
On Saint John's Night
My iron rod
My dawn hat
For me to go cowpunching
On Saint Peter's Night
My dawn hat
My lasso
For me to go cowpunching
On Saint Mark's Night
What a sad day I had today
Sadder that I am now
To see our ox dead
On this lady's door step
Being a poor vaqueiro
Wondering in the land covered by
  Second growth I found our ox
It died from maggot-filled sores
Being a poor vaqueiro
Camping here and there
I left on Monday
Arived in the middle of the week
Sendo en pobre vaqueiro
Que andou na vaqueijada
Encontrei o nosso boi
Ele morreu na malhada

ME FAZEM UM SILÊNCIO

Amo:

Eh! Primeiro Vaqueiro! (falado)

1o Vaqueiro:

Gente me fazem um silêncio
Eu ouvi meu Amo chamar
Não sei se é pra meu bem
Não sei se é pra meu mau

Amo:

Eh! Primeiro Vaqueiro! (falado)

1o Vaqueiro:

Meu Amo quando me chama
Meu cavalo estava solto
Estava dormindo e sonhando
Que o nosso boi era morto

Amo:

Eh! Primeiro Vaqueiro! (falado)
Being a poor vaqueiro
Taking care of cattle in the field
I found our ox
Dead under the shadow of large trees

PEOPLE QUIET PLEASE

Master:

Eh! First Vaqueiro! (spoken)

1st Vaqueiro:

People keep quiet
I hear my Master calling
I don't know if it is for good
I don't know if it is for bad

Master:

Eh! First Vaqueiro! (spoken)

1st Vaqueiro:

My Master when you called
My horse was loose
I was sleeping and dreaming

That our ox was dead

Master:

Eh! First Vaqueiro! (spoken)

1o Vaqueiro:

Meu Amo quando me chama
Eu estava na hora de sair
O portão estava fechado
Eu não podia sair
Eu ouvi tropeis de cavalo
Eu vim por aqui
Pensava de ser meu Amo
Que vinha atrás de mim
Eu ouvi tropeis de cavalo
Eu ouvi for a bater
Pensava de ser meu Amo
Que vinha pra me prender
Boa noite senhor meu Amo
Como está, como passou
Aqui está seu bom vaqueiro
Pra que meu Amo chamou
Boa noite senhor meu Amo
Com está, como passou
Aqui está seu bom vaqueiro
Pra que meu Amo queria

1st Vaqueiro:

My master when you called
I was getting ready to come
The gate was closed
I could not get out
I heard trumping of the horse
And I came this way
I thought that it was my Master
Who was coming after me
I heard tramping of the horse
And I heard knocking out there
I thought that it was my Master
Who was coming to get me
Good night Lord my Master
How are you, how have you been
Here is your good vaqueiro
Why have you called
Good night Lord my Master
How are you, how have you been
Here is your good vaqueiro
What did my Master want
Boa noite senhor meu Amo
Como passou, como está
Aqui está seu bom vaqueiro
Pra que você precizar
Boa noite senhor meu Amo
Eu quem sou seu empregado
Aqui está seu bom vaqueiro
Pra que você precizar

Amo:

Vaqueiro sela meu cavalo
Até de selar o teu
Eu quero vencer demanda
Que o jigante não venceu

1o Vaqueiro:

Meu Amo você não sabe
Que seu cavalo morreu
Estava no campo pastando
Foi quando a cobra bateu

Amo:

Vaqueiro não diz tal coisa
Eu fico arrenegado
Se meu Jurema morreu
Sela meu Rosto Queimado
Good night Lord my Master
How have you been, how are you
Here is your good vaqueiro
For whatever you desire
Good night Lord my Master
It's me your employee
Here is your good vaqueiro
For whatever you need

APPENDIX 2

Master:

Vaqueiro saddle my horse
Saddle even yours
I want to win the plea
That the giant did not win

1st Vaqueiro:

My Master don't you know
That your horse died?
It was grazing in the field
And the snake bit it

Master:

Vaqueiro don't say such thing
That I become very angry
If my whit ehorse (jurema) is dead
Then saddle my brown one

10 Vaqueiro:

Meu Amo Você não sabe
Que seu selim está trocado
Selim que sela Jurema
Não sela Rosto Queimado

Amo:

Vaqueiro tu vai lá em casa
Lá em casa na varanda
Vai buscar meu livro mestre
Eu quero vencer demanda

10 Vaqueiro:

Meu Amo eu fui em sua casa
Dei um avolta na varanda
Não achei seu livro mestre
Livro de vencer demanda

Amo:

Vaqueiro tu vai lá en casa
Na gaveta mais pequena
Vai buscar meu livro mestre
Tinteiro, papel, e pena

10 Vaqueiro:

Meu Amo eu já fui, já vem
Lá na gaveta pequena
O tinteiro estava seco
Não achei papel nem pena

1st Vaqueiro:

My Master don't you know
That your English saddle is changed
Saddle that saddles white horse
Does not saddle the brown horse

Master:

Vaqueiro go there to my house
And look around on the veranda
Go bring me my book of prayers
I want to conquer the plea

1st Vaqueiro:

My Master I went to your house
And looked around on the veranda
I didn't find your book of prayers
With which to conquer the plea

Master:

Vaqueiro go there in the house
In the smallest drawer
Go and bring my book of prayers
Ink pot, paper, and pen

1st Vaqueiro:

My Master I went and came back
There in the smallest drawer
The ink pot was dry
I didn't find paper or pen
Meu Amo eu já fui, já vem
Nada deste eu encontrei
Encontrei Dona Maria
E com ela eu conversei

APPENDIX 2

Amo:

Dezangado que estou hoje
Eu te dou comm este ferão
Se o ferão não te ofendeu
Vaqueiro tu tens razão

1o Vaqueiro:

Minha patroa me acuida
Que meu Amo quer me dar
Por caso do nosso boi
Que não dormiu no curral

Dona Maria:

Sendo eu Dona Maria
Mulher de grande cautela
Não se maltrata um vaqueiro
Nesta fazenda eu não quero
Te ajoelha me vaqueiro
Joelha e pedi perdão
Que eu tenho o anél de ouro
Para tua livracão
My master I went and came back
None of these have I found
I found Dona Maria
And conversed with her

Master:

How annoyed I am today
I'll hit you with this iron rod
If the iron rod does not hurt you
Coyboy, you are right

1st Vaqueiro:

My Lady help me
My Master want to hit me
Because of our ox
Which didn't sleep in the corral

Dona Maria:

Being Dona Maria
Woman of great care

One does not mistreat a vaqueiro
On this ranch, I don't allow
Kneel my vaqueiro
Kneel and ask forgiveness
I have a golden ring
For your freedom
Tu não chora meu vaqueiro
Que teu Amo não (vai) te dar
Eu dou um abraco nele
Ele vai te perdoar

1o Vaqueiro:

Minha patroa me diga
Que seu vaqueiro é bonito
Montado em meu cavalo
Com meu lacinho de fita

Dona Maria:

Vaqueiro tu não és bonito
Porque teu Amo não quer
Tenho uma caixinha de ouro
Toda coberta de anél
Te alevanta meu vaqueiro
Levanta do frio chão
Eu quem sou Dona Maria
Espousa do teu patrão
Te alevanta meu vaqueiro
Dá uma volta pro-cu-lá
Vai aprocura do boi
Na porteira do curral
Don't cry my vaqueiro
Your Master will not hit you
I'll give him a hug
And he will forgive you

1st Vaqueiro:

My Lady tell me
That you vaqueiro is beautiful
Riding on my horse
With my little ribbon bow

Dona Maria:

Vaqueiro you are not beautiful
Because your Master does not want
I have a golden little box
All covered with rings
Arise my vaqueiro
Arise from the cold ground
I am Dona Maria
Your Master's spouse
Arise my vaqueiro
Go over there
To look for the ox
At the gate of the corral

1o Vaqueiro:

Ajoelhei com a tristesa
Me levantei com alegria
No céu tem um Deus por mim
Na terra é Dona Maria

1st Vaqueiro:

I kneeled with sadness
But I rised with happiness
There is a God in the heaven for me
And on earth, Dona Maria

GLOSSARY

Agrado. Same as *Capim*

Amo. The owner of the ox and the ranch where the story takes place.

Apreparo. Props. The term is also used for participants' costumes that are ready for use.

Arco. The authentic bow carried by the indigenous characters in the Bumba-meu-Boi of Pindaré/Viana.

Baiado. The choreography for the ox and participants.

Bailado. The term is used to designate the dance performed by participants during the presentation of the Boi.

Bailante. Bumba-meu-Boi participant; same as *Brincante*.

Balaiada. A rebellion led by Manuel Francisco dos Anjos Ferreira (known as Balião), which began in 1838 and was ended in the district of Caxias, Maranhão, in 1841 by the national army under the command of Luis Alve de Lima e Silva. De Lima e Silva was then given the noble title of "Duc of Caxias" by President Vicente Pires de Camargo, and was immortalized as the Patron of the Brazilian armed forces after his successful campaign in the Paraguaian war; see also Serra, Astolfo.

Barra. The skirt sewn to the ox frame.

Baseado. Something beautiful, rich. This is often used in reference to the quality of the actual presentation of the Boi.

Batalhão. A Bumba-meu-Boi troupe.

Bateria. Accompanying musical ensemble composed primarily of percussive instruments.

Batismo. The initial feast that takes place on June 23, presenting the ox to Saint John with songs and prayers to the saint. This is an influence from the *Tambor de Mina*, attested by the rhythm and the use of an incense burner.

Batuque. The total sound produced by a Bumba-meu-Boi troupe during the presentation. The term is also used in reference to the accompanying musical ensemble.

Boi. A frame in shape of an ox made of wood from the *geniparama* or *paparaúba* and *buriti* trees of the palm family, covered with black or navy blue velour adorned with embroidery of iconographic motif made with colorful glass beads, and mirrors. The term Boi is also a short appellation of the actual Bumba-meu-Boi.

Boiar. To participate in Bumba-meu-Boi; to sing a Bumba-meu-Boi song.

Boiada. A generic term used in Maranhão to designate the period during which Bumba-meu-Boi is celebrated. The term is also employed in reference to the actual presentation of the Boi.

Boi-da-Ilha. The Island (São Luis) style of Bumba-meu-Boi. See also *Boi de Matraca*.

Boi-de-Brincar. An expression used in São Francisco section of São Luis in reference to the Bumba-meu-Boi organized without special reasons.

Boi-de-Matraca. Same as *Boi da Ilha*, it identifies a Bumba-meu-Boi style in which the musical instrument *Matraca* is the main instrument.

Boi-de-Pancadaria. A style of Bumba-meu-Boi in which the orchestration is composed of a combination of the *zabumba* drums, large tambourines, a large friction drum known as *tambor onça* (wildcat drum), tin can rattles, and cowbells with flap.

Boi-de-Promessa. The performance of Bumba-meu-Boi organized to keep a promise.

Boi Estrela. Literally, the Star Ox. A name given to the Master's favorite ox in the legend to distinguish it from the rest of the herd.

Botar. To organize or to contract a performance of Bumba-meu-Boi.

Braçadeira. Ankle and wristband made of feathers worn by the *Caboclo Real* (royal indigenous person) in the *Boi de Matraca* and *Boi da Ilha* styles.

Branco. White. The owner of the house where the presentation of the Boi is held.

Brincadeira. Amusement, merry-making, often used in reference to the actual presentation of the Boi.

Brincante. Participant of Bumba-meu-Boi.

Brincar. To dance or participate in the presentation of Bumba-meu-Boi.

Bumbá. An interjection of invitation to dance.

Bumba-meu-Boi. Literally, "dance-my-ox."

Burrinha. Small frame of *buriti* and *cipó* wood made in the shape of a grotesque donkey. It differs from that of the ox by having an opening on the dorsal of the frame to allow the participant to wear it as a skirt around his waist that is secured with a pair of suspenders. The *Burrinha* frame is covered with a colorful cloth, but lacks decorations.

Cabéceira. In the *Zabumba* style, the term is used for the *Amo*, the leader of the troupe. The same term also designates the opening song led by the *Amo*.

Cabôclo. Indigenous person in Bumba-meu-Boi. Often pronounced *cabôco*.

Cabôclo-de-Fita. Same as *Rajado*, a term used in the *Zabumba* style for the vaqueiros with large hats covered with long colorful ribbons.

Cabôclo-de-Pena. See *Caboclo Real*.

Cabôclo Real. Royal indigenous person whose function in the drama includes the imprisonment of *Nêgo Chico*. They number from three to twenty in a troupe. Their costumes are lavishly made with feathers and include hat, shoulder cap, skirt, ankle and wristbands, and bow and arrow.

Caipora. Enormous dolls used in some styles of the Bumba-meu-Boi to scare children.

Caixa-do-Boi. A rehearsal session of the Bumba-meu-Boi.

Cantador. The composer or the leader of song.

Canzá. An indigenous Brazilian musical instrument consisting of a length of bamboo with notches cut along the side, over which a stick is rubbed to produce the sound. This instrument is also popular among urban musicians in Angola. The same instrument is also known in Brazil by the names of *reco-reco*, *caracaxa*, and *querequere*. This instrument is found depicted in "La Promenade du Dimanche Aprés-midi" painting by Jean-Baptiste Debret (cf. "Die Baducca in São Paulo" in C. F. von Martins & J. B. von Pix's *Atlas zur Reise in Brasilien, 1817-1820*).

Capacete. Specific name of the feather hat used by the "royal" indigenous people in the *Matraca* style.

Capim. The payment for the presentation of the Boi.

Catirina. Pai Francisco's wife. This character is traditionally played by a male dressed up as a female. In Maranhão, some troupes are using females to play this role.

Cazumba. The masked characters in the Bumba-meu-Boi. They are believed by some writers to represent African mystical spirits.

Chapeu de Fita. The hat made of ribbons used by cowboys in the *Zabumba* style. See *Rajado*.

Chico. A nickname for Pai Francisco and *Nêgo Chico*.

Congaceiros. Outlaws who lived in Northern Brazil at the turn of the century. The most celebrated of these was called Lampião.

Contra-Amo. The *Amo*'s assistant.

Cordão. Literally, twine or string. In Bumba-meu-Boi, it identifies a dance format adopted by a troupe.

Corrida. A round of *cachaça* (sugarcane rum) or *tiquira* (casava/manioc rum).

Couro. The ox's hide made of black or navy blue velour decorated with iconographic representation of the troupe's theme for the year.

Desafio. A verbal challenge between singers of the same or different troupes. The challenge was formulated according to unwritten poetic rules similar to those established in the Northeast by Lampião and his followers at the turn of the century.

Descanso. The stick used by the *Zabumba* players to rest their drums on during the performance.

Desgarrada. See *Desafio*.

Despedida. Farewell. The last song sung at the "killing of the ox" performance. Its subject matter deals primarily with longing and departure.

Espritado. A good singer. The term designates also a funny character.

Foriquilha. Same as *Descanso*.

Francisco, Pai. Leading character in the drama. The slave on the ranch who kills the master's favorite ox.

Guarneção. The act of gathering

Guarnecer. To gather, roundup, or to get ready.

Guarnecido. In the *Matraca* style, *guarnecido* is used in reference to a strong *Matraca* accompaniment or to comment on how the rhythmic patterns of the instruments are well interlocked.

Joelheira. Knee braces made of feathers worn by "royal indigenous people" in the *Matraca* style.

Ladainha. A collection of prayers and songs of praise sung to Saint John during the baptism and the death of the ox performances.

Lança. A prop spear carried by the dancing indigenous people.

Lá Vai. A song performed after the authorization to inform the owner of the house where the presentation of the Bumba-meu-Boi is going to take place.

Licença. A song sung near the place with the presentation of the Boi is going to take place, requesting permission to approximate.

Machucado. An individual style of dancing.

Mãe Catirina. See Catirina.

Maracá. A tin-can rattle usually played by the *Cazumbá*, Dona Maria and her assistants, and the *Amo*.

Matança. A section of the drama in which the actual dramatization of the legend is carried out. It is during this section that the symbolic killing and resurrection are dramatized. This term also refers to the last performance of the season *Matança do Boi* after which the ox is dissected and the meat symbolically distributed or sold among those present.

Matraca. Originally, *matraca* was the name given to a sistrum-like shaker made of small pieces of wood. In Maranhão, the term refers to a pair of wood blocks that are hand held and clapped together to produce the desired rhythmic pattern. The same term is also used to designate the style of a Bumba-meu-Boi troupe in which this instrument predominates, such as in the Pindaré and Viana styles.

Matracão. A large sized wooden rhythm blocks played by participants in the *Boi da Ilha* and *Boi de Viola* styles. *Matracão* (pl. *matracões*).

Miolo. The name given to the individual who hides inside the ox's frame and dances with it.

Molhado. A performance during which participants drank plenty of *cachaça* (sugarcane rum) and *tiquira* (cassava/manioc rum).

Mourão. A tree trunk half buried in the center of the presentation ground to which the ox is tied on the day of the killing.

Morte. Death of the ox designates the last performance of the season. During this session, the ox meat is symbolically distributed or sold among those present.

Murrada. The sound of the troupe during the presentation. In the early period of the Bumba-meu-Boi, *murrada* was also a form of challenge between opposing troupes. The troupe that is overpowered *foi abafado* (has been baffled by the noise).

Mutuca. Women who accompany the troupe. They look after the rum, the decoration of the ox's hide, and participants' costumes.

Nêgo Chico. See Pai Francisco; Francisco.

Orquestra. The European style of the Bumba-meu-Boi characterized by the use of cordophones (*cavaquinho*, guitar) and aerophones (trumpet, trombone) instruments of the western origin.

Pai Francisco. See Francisco, and *Nêgo Chico*.

Panda. See *tinideira*.

Pandeirão. A large sized hand drum measuring approximately 36 inches in diameter whose frame is made of plywood and the head is goatskin. *Pandeirão* (pl. *pandeirões*) is used in the Island style of the Boi.

Pandeirinho. A small sized hand drum made of the *genipapo* wood and covered with *cutia*'s skin. This drum is used in he Pindaré/Viana styles and in that of *Zabumba*.

Peneiro. The complete costume of the "royal indigenous person." The term is also used in reference to the royal indigenous person himself.

Peitoral. Shoulder cap/vest made of black or navy blue velour adorned with colorful motifs, worn by participants in all styles.

Pesado. That which is good, well rehearsed.

Pindaré/Viana. Styles of Bumba-meu-Boi, in the townships by the same name, characterized by the use of *matraca*, *pandeirinho*, feathered hats, and a slow tempo rhythm.

Pique. Name given to bloody encounters between Bumba-meu-Boi troupes.

Polainas. White spats used in the *Zabumba* style.

Puxar. To play the friction drum or to lead singing.

Rajado. In the *Zabumba* style the *rajados* are those participants with large hats covered with long ribbons.

Rapazes. Young men in the presentation. They play the role of intermediaries between the *Amo* and Pai Francisco, and between the *Amo* and the Indigenous people.

Rebanho. The home base where the troupe rehearses. Often this is the site where the ox is baptized at the first performance of the season and killed at the last.

Saióte. A small skirt of black or navy blue decorated velour worn by participants in the Orchestra and the Pindaré/Viana styles.

Seco. *Boi seco* is a presentation of Bumba-meu-Boi where there is little or nothing to drink.

Sotaque. Generic term for styles of Bumba-meu-Boi. The term can also be used to refer to linguistic accent.

Surrar. A rudimentary form of drum made from a tree trunk (*siriba* or white *manão*) hollowed with fire and covered with raw cowhide which is fixed to the drumhead with wooden pegs. This drum is common in the *Boi de Zabumba* style.

Tamborim. High pitched single-headed, square shaped hand drum played with a stick.

Tambor onça. Wildcat-drum is a friction drum with an internal shaft. It is made of a hollowed tree trunk covered at one end with goat or skin. The shaft is fixed to the center of the skin. This instrument derives its name from the sound it produces which resembles the ox or the bellowing of a wildcat. When used in the context of samba music, similar instrument is called *cuíca*.

Tanga. A small skirt used by participants in Bumba-meu-Boi. See also *Saióte*.

Tanga de Pena. A small skirt made of feathers worn by "royal indigenous people" the *Matraca* and the Island styles.

Tanger. To organize, sponsor, or finance the performance of Bumba-meu-Boi.

Terreiro. The grounds where the performance of Bumba-meu-Boi is held.

Tinideira. Large frame single-headed hand drum.

Tirar. To compose a song—*toada*

Toada. According to the *Novo Dicionário Aurelio*, *toada* signifies rumor or hearsay. The same source also defines *toada* as any ballad with a simple and monotonous melody, short text, sentimental or mischievous, with verses and refrains. In Bumba-meu-Boi, both meanings apply, songs improvised during the performance of Bumba-meu-Boi.

Tripa. See *Miólo*.

Urrou. The *toada* (song) which announces the ox's resurrection and the beginning of the feast.

Vaqueiro. Cowboy. See also *Rajado*.

Vaqueirada. A group of *vaqueiros* during the performance of Bumba-meu-Boi.

Vara. A stick, generally from the *geniparana* tree, decorated with colored-paper and flowers that the *Rajados* and vaqueiros carry during the performance of the Boi.

Vadiar. To dance or participate in

Bumba-meu-Boi.

Viola. A guitar-like chordophone. The most common viola has 10 strings tuned in pairs. There are several tunings of the viola, but the most common of them is 1) Cebolão in D-d-f#-a-d; 1.1) Cebolão in E-b-g-b-e; 2) Natural, which follows guitar tuning a-d-g-b-e; and 3) Rio Abaixo g-d-g-b-d.

Zabumba. This term designates both the drum similar to the bass drum, and the African style of the Boi in which this drum is prominent. The term is also used to refer to the rhythmic pattern played on this drum.

BIBLIOGRAPHY

"A Morte do Bumba-meu-Boi." *O Globo,* 21 de junho de 1955, São Luís, Maranhão.

Almeida, Renato. "Brazilian Folk Patterns." *Americas.* 4 (March, 1952): 28-30.

_____. "O Bumba-meu-Boi de Camassari." *Cultura Política.* Ano II, 19 (1942): 193-197.

_____. *Tablado Folclórico.* São Paulo: Recordi Brasileira, 1961.

Alvarenga, Oneyda. *Música Popular Brasilena.* Buenos Aires: Fundo de Cultura Econômica, 1947.

_____. *Música Popular Brasilena.* São Paulo: Duas Cidades, 1982.

Amaral Junior, Amadeu. "Reisado, Bumba-meu-Boi e Pastoris." *Revista do Arquivo Municipal de São Paulo.* VI, 64 (Fevereiro de 1940): 273-281.

Andrade, Lauro Ruiz de. *Bumba-meu-Boi e Outros Temas.* Fortaleza: Edições Universidade Federal de Ceará, 1985.

Andrade, Mário de. "As Danças Dramáticas do Brasil." *Boletim Latino-Americano de Música.* Ano VI, Tomo VI (Abril de 1946): 49-97.

Araújo, Alceu Maynard. *Cultura Popular Brasileira.* São Paulo: Melhoramentos, 1977.

Araújo, Maria do Socorro. *Tu Contas! Eu Conto! Caracterização e Significado do Bumba-meu-Boi para a População do Bairro da Madre de Deus, como Expressão da Cultura Popular e como Lazer em São Luis.* São Luis: Serviço de Imprensa e Obras Gráficas do Estado, 1986.

Athayde, Jacy de Mattos. "Tutoia-Velha sem"Bumba-meu-Boi" é uma Cidade Triste no Maranhão." *Jornal do Comercio.* Caderno 1 (14 Agosto de 1966): 3.

A Voz Paraense. Ano I, 3 (1850): 1.

Azevedo, Arthur. "O Bumba-meu-Boi." *Kosmos.* Ano III, 1 (1906).

Azevedo, Fernando Correa de. "O Boi-de-Mamão no Litoral Paranaense." *Revista Brasileira de Folclore. Ano III, 6 (Maio/Agosto de 1963): 113-124.

Azevedo Neto, Américo. *Bumba-meu-Boi no Maranhão*. São Luis: Alcântara, 1983.

_____. *Bumba-meu-Boi no Maranhão*. São Luis: Alumar, 1997.

Barroso, Gustavo. *Ao Som da Viola*. 2a. ed. Rio de Janeiro: Departamento de Imprensa Nacional, 1949.

Bastide, Roger. *Les Amériques Noires*. Paris: Petite Bibliothèque Payot, 1967.

Beattie, John. *Other Cultures: Aims, Methods and Achievements in Social Anthropology*. New York: Free Press of Glencoe, 1964.

Beaurepaire-Rohan, Henrique de. *Dicionário de Vocabulos Brasileiros*. 2a. ed. Salvador: Livraria Progresso, 1956.

Bettencourt, Gastão de. *O Folclore no Brasil*. Salvador: Publicações da Universidad da Bahia, 1957.

Boiteux, José Arthur. *Águas Passadas*. 2a. ed. Florianópolis: Livraria Central, 1932.

_____. *Arcaz de um Barriga-Verde e Águas Passadas*. Florianópolis: Editora da Universidade Federal de Santa Catarina, 1993.

Borba Filho, Hermilo. *Apresentação do Bumba-meu-Boi*. Recife: Imprensa Universitaria, 1967.

Brandão, Théo. *Bumba-meu-Boi*. Maceió: Universidade Federal de Alagoas, Museu Théo Brandão, 1976.

Bueno, André Paula. *Bumba-Boi Maranhense em São Paulo*. São Paulo: Nankin Editorial, 2001.

"Bumba, meu Boi!" *A Ilha*. (6 de Junho de 1976).

"Bumba-Bois Realizam o 'Batizado'." *O Imparcial*. (24 de Junho de 1976).

Campello, Samuel. "Fizeram os Negros Teatro no Brasil?" in *Novos Estudos Afro-Brasileiros* edited by Gilberto Freyre e outros. Rio de Janeiro: Civilização Brasileira, 1937, pp. 222-242.

Canjão, Isanda Maria Falcão. "Bumba-meu-Boi: O Rito Pede 'Passagem' em São Luis do Maranhão." Porto Alegre, Universidade Federal de Rio Grande de Sul – Dissertação de Mestrado em Antropologia, 2001.

Cardozo, Joaquim. "Bumba-meu-Boi Maranhense." *Módulo*. (Agosto de 1955).

_____. *De uma Noite de Festa: Bumba-meu-Boi em Três Quadros*. Rio de Janeiro: Livraria Agir, 1971.

_____. *O Coronel de Macambira: Bumba-meu-Boi, em Dois Quadros*. Rio de Janeiro: Editôra Civilização Brasileira, 1963.

Carneiro, Edison. *A Negros Bantus*. Rio de Janeiro: Civilização Brasileira, 1937.

_____. *Sabedoria Popular*. Rio de Janeiro: Instituto Nacional do Livro, 1957

_____. *Folguedos Tradicionais*. Rio de Janeiro: Conquista, 1974.

Carvalho, José Rodrigues de. *Cancioneiro do Norte*. 3a. ed. Rio de Janeiro: Instituto Nacional do Livro, 1967.

Carvalho, Maria Michol Pinho de. *Matracas que Desafiam o Tempo: E o Bumba-meu-Boi do Maranhão*. São Luis: n.p., 1995.

Cascudo, Luis da Câmara. "Bumba-meu-Boi." In *Dicionário do Folclore Brasileiro*. 2a. ed. Rio de Janeiro: Ministério da Educação e Cultura, Instituto Nacional do Livro, 1954.

_____. "Zabumba," in *Dicionário do Folclore Brasileiro*. 2a. ed. Rio de Janeiro: Instituto Nacional do Livro – Ministério da Educação e Cultura, 1962, p. 791.

_____. *Antologia do Folclore Brasileira: Séculos XVI-XVII-XVIII. Os Cronistas Coloniais. Os Viajantes Estrangeiros. Bibliografia e Notas*. 3a ed.. Primeiro Volume. São Paulo: Livraria Martins Editora, 1965.

_____. "Tourinhas," in *Dicionario do Folclore Brasileiro*. 4a ed. São Paulo: Edições Melhoramentos, 1979, p. 758.

Castelo Branco, R. P. *A Civilização do Couro*. Teresina: Departamento Estadual de Imprensa e Propaganda, 1942.

Chaves, Luis. "Bumba-meu-Boi" do Brasil: "Tourinhas" de Portugal." *Ocidente*. LVI, 254 (Junho de 1959): 352-354.

Conklin, Harold. "Lexicographical Treatment of Folk Taxonomies." *International Journal of American Linguistics*. 28, 2 (April, 1962): 119-141.

Costa, Dias da. *O Bumba-meu-Boi*. Rio de Janeiro: Campanha de Defesa do Folclore Brasileiro, 1973.

Costa, F. A. Pereira da. *Folclore Pernambucano*. Recife: Arquivo Público Estadual, 1974.

Costa, Ivan Sarney. "O Bumba de Noso Boi." *O Estado do Maranhão*. (17 de Junho de 1973).

Coutinho Filho, Francisco. *Violas e Repentes*. Recife: Saraiva, 1953.

Da Matta, R. "Constraint and License: a Preliminary Study of two Brazilian National Rituals," in *Secular Ritual.* Moore, Sally F. and Myerhoff, Barbara G. Amsterdam: Van Gorcum, 1977, pp. 244-264.

Debret, Jean Baptiste. *Viagem Pitoresca e Histórica ao Brasil.* São Paulo: Editora da Universidade de São Paulo, 1972.

Diario da Manha. São Luis, Maranhão, July 1, 17 de 1965.

Diegues Junior, Manuel. "O Bumba-meu-Boi." *Revista Brasileira de Geografia.* XXI, 1 (1959): 111-113.

Diniz, Luzandra. "A Participação Feminina no Bumba-meu-Boi do Maranhão," in *Comisão Maranhense de Folclore.* Boletim 10/Junho 1998, p.12.

Dornas Filho, João. *Achegas de Etnografia e Folclore.* Belo Horizonte: Imprensa/ Publicações, 1972.

Drama e Fetiche: Vodum, Bumba-meu-Boi e Samba no Benin. Rio de Janeiro: Centro Nacional de Folclore e Cultura Popular – FUNARTE, 1998.

Duarte, Abelardo. *Um Folguedo do Povo: O Bumba-meu-Boi, Ensaio de Historia e Folclore.* Maceió: Edições Caeté, 1957.

Echezona, W. Wilberforce. *Nigerian Musical Instruments: A Definitive Catalogue.* Lansing: The Apollo Publishers, 1981.

Falcão, Cyro. *Bumba-meu-Boi do Maranhão.* São Luis: Universidade Federal do Maranhão, s.d.

Ferreira, Alexandre Rodrigues. *Viagem Filosófica pelas Capitanias do Grão Pará, Rio Negro, Mato Groso e Cuiabá.* Rio de Janeiro: Conselho Federal de Cultura, s.d.

Ferreira, Ascenso. "O Bumba-meu-Boi." *Arquivos, Prefeitura Municipal do Recife.* no. 1-2 (1944): 1-15.

Ferretti, Sergio Figueiredo, ed. *Tambor de Crioula: Ritual e Espetaculo.* São Luis: Serviço de Imprensa e Obras Gráficas do Estado, 1979.

França, Jeovah Silva. "O Meu Bumba-meu-Boi." *Cultura Popular* (Julho de 1981): 37-50.

Frazer, Sir James George. *The Golden Bough: A Study in Magic and Religion.* 2nd ed. London: The McMillan, 1900.

Frobenius, Leo. "The Origin of African Civilization," in *Smithsonian Institution Annual Report 1898.* Washington, D.C.: Smithsonian, 1898.

Fundação Movimento Brasileiro de Alfabetização. *Mapa Cultural.* Vol. I. Rio de Janeiro: Ministério da Educação, 1980.

Galvão, E. "Boi Bumba: Versão do Baixo Amazonas." *Anhembi*. Vol. III, 8 (1951): 277-291.

Gama, Padre Lopes. "A Estulotice do Bumba-meu-Boi." *O Carapuceiro*. no. 2 (11 de Janeiro de 1840).

Gay, Conego João Pedro. *História da República Jesuitica do Paraguai: Desde Descobrimento do Rio da Prata até aos nossos Dias, Ano de 1861*. Segunda Ediição. Rio de Janiro: Imprensa Nacional, 1942.

Gomes, Laura Graziela Figueiredo Fernandes., Livia Barbosa, and José Augusto Drummond. *O Brasil não é para Principiantes: Carnavais, Malandros e Heróis, 20 Anos Depois*. 2 ed. Rio de Janeiro: Editora Fundação Getúlio Vargas, 2001.

Gottheim, Vivian I. "Bumba-meu-Boi, a Musical Play from Maranhão." *The World of Music*. XXX, 2 (1988): 40-67.

_____. Eve of Saint John's Day: A Work in Words and Images Based on an Aesthetic Inquiry Into the Dramatic-Dance "Bumba-meu-Boi" As Presented in São Luis of Maranhão, Brazil. Thesis (D.A.) New York University, 1984.

Goulart, J. A. *Brasil do Boi e do Couro*. Vol. I & II. Rio de Janeiro: Edições GRD, 1966.

Griz, Jayme. *Gentes, Coisas e Cantos do Nordeste*. Recife: Arquivo Público Estadual, 1954.

Harap, Louis. *Social Roots of the Arts*. New York: International Publishers, 1949.

Hill, Errol. *The Trinidad Carnival: Mandate for a National Theatre.* Austin: University of Texas Press, 1972.

Hymes, Dell. *Foundations in Sociolinguistics: an Ethnographic Approach*. Philadelphia: University of Pennsylvania Press, 1974.

_____. "Models of the Interaction of Language and Social Life," in Gumperz, J.J. and Hymes, Dell, eds. *Directions in Sociolinguistics: the Ethnography of Communication.* New York: Holt, Rinehart and Winston, 1972, pp. 35-71.

Jornal Pequeno. São Luis, Maranhão, June 23, 1966.

Kazadi wa Mukuna. "Bumba-meu-Boi in Maranhão," in *Brasilien. Einfuhrung in Musikkulturen Brasiliens*. Tiago de Oliveira Pinto, ed. Mainz: Schott, 1986, pp. 108-120.

_____. *Contribuição Bantu na Música Popular Brasileira*. São Paulo: Global Editora, [1979].

_____. *Contribuição Bantu na Música Popular Brasileira: Perspectivas*

Etnomusicológicas. São Paulo: Terceira Margem, 2000.

_____. "Creative Practice in African Music: New Perspectives in the Scrutiny of Africanisms in Diaspora." *Black Music Research Journal.* 17, 2 (Fall 1997): 239-250.

_____. "Sotaques: Style and Ethnicity in a Brazilian Folk Drama," in *Music and Black Ethnicity: The Caribbean and South America.* Gérard H. Béhague, ed. New Brunswick: Transaction Publishers, 1994, pp. 207-224.

_____. "The Process of Assimilation of African Musical Elements in Brazil." *The World of Music.* 32, 3 (1990): 104-106.

_____. "The Rise of Bumba-meu-Boi in Maranhão: Resilience of African-Brazilian Cultural Identity," in *Black Brazil: Culture, Identity, and Social Mobilization.* Larry Crook and Randal Johnson, eds. Los Angeles: University of California at Los Angeles Latin American Center Publication, 2000, pp. 297-310.

_____. "'Nsumwinu': Meaning and Role in the Structural Composition of Melodies in the Urban Music of the Democratic Republic of the Congo." *África: Revista de Centro de Estudos Africanos, Número Especial 2012: África Única e Plural – Melanges em Homenagem ao Professor Fernando Augusto Albuquerque Mourão*, Organizador Kabengele Munanga - Universidade de São Paulo, Brasil, 2012, pp. 199-210.

Kazadi wa Mukuna and Tiago de Oliveira Pinto. "The Study of African Musical Contribution to Latin America and the Caribbean: A Methodological Guideline." A paper developed in collaboration with the "Grupo de Trabalho – CIDEM." *The World of Music* 32, 3 (1990): 103-104.

Kubik, Gerhard. *Angolan Traits in Black Music, Games and Dances of Brazil: A Study of African Cultural Extensions overseas.* Lisboa: Junta de Investigações Científicas do Ultramar, 1979.

_____. *Extensionen Afrikanischer Kulturen in Brasilien.* Aachen: Alano, Ed. Herodot, 1991.

_____. . "Mãe Catirina's Desire: Psychoanalytic Reflections on the Legend of Bumba-meu-Boi, Brazil" *Psychoanalytic Review* 95 (6), (December 2008): 1035-1044.

Lamas, Dulce Martins. "Boi Bumba e Passaros." *Revista Brasileira de Folclore.* Ano VIII, 20 (Janeiro/Abril de 1968): 33-42.

Laytano, Dante de. *Origens do Folclore Brasileiro.* Segunda Edição. Rio de Janeiro: Campanha de Defesa do Folclore Brasileiro, 1971.

Levi-Strauss, Claude. *Totemism.* Boston: Beacon Press, 1963.

Lima, Carlos de. *Bumba-meu-Boi*. São Luis: Fundo Rotativo de Incentivo ao Turismo (FURINTUR), 1968.

_____. *Bumba-meu-Boi do Maranhão*. São Luis: Fundo Rotativo de Incentivo ao Turismo (FURINTUR), 1969.

_____. *Bumba-meu-Boi*. Terceira Edição. São Luis: Editora Augusta, 1982.

_____. "Universo do Bumba-meu-Boi." *Comissão Maranhense de Folclore*. Boletim 11/Agosto de 1998, pp. 8-9.

Lima, Mesquitela. *Antropologia do Simbólico ou o Simbólico da Antropologia*. Porto: Editorial Presença, 1983.

Lima, Rossini Tavares de. *Abece do Folclore*. Quarta Edição. São Paulo: Ricordi, 1968.

_____. *Folclore das Festas Cíclicas*. São Paulo: Irmãos Vitale, 1971.

_____. *Folguedos Populares do Brasil: Maracatu, Congada, Moçambique, Reisado, Guerreiro, Folia de Reis, Dança dos Tapuios, Cabocolinhos, Calapó, Bumba-meu-Boi e Outros Folguedos do Boi, Chegança e Fandango ou Marujada*. São Paulo: Ricordi, 1962.

Lowie, Robert H. *The History of Ethnological Theory*. New York: Holt, Rinehart and Winston, 1937.

Luna, Mário Roso de. *El Simbolismo de las Reliqiones del Mundo y el Problema de la Fidelidad*. Madrid: Editorial EYRAS, 1977.

Macedo, Eurico Telles de. *O Maranhão e suas Riquezas*. Salvador: n.p., 1947.

Macedo, José Norberto. *Fazendas de Gado no Vale do São Francisco*. Rio de Janeiro: Ministério da Agricultura, 1952.

Mahiri, Jelani K. "Of Ox, Slaves, Cowboys and Indians: Plot, Performance and Power in the Bumba-meu-Boi of Brazil," unpublished manuscript

Maranhão, Departamento de Cultura. *Bumba-meu-Boi do Maranhão*. São Luis: Departamento de Cultura do Maranhão, 1967.

Marques, Ester. *Midia e Experiencia Estética na Cultura Popular: O Caso do Bumba-meu-Boi*. São Luis: Imprensa Universitaria, 1999.

Marques, Nubia. "Centros de Tradição e Cultura." *Revista Sergipana de Folclore*. Ano I, 1 (Agosto de 1976): 17-33.

Martins, Rosa Mochel. "Bumba-meu-Boi: História, Maravilha, Fantasia." Miniografia. São Luis: Departamento da Secretária de Educação e Ação Comunitária da Prefeitura de São Luis, 1974.

Masson, Nonnato. "A Morte do Bumba-meu-Boi." *O Globo*. São Luis, 21 de Junho de 1955.

Maultsby, Portia K. "Africanisms in African-American Music," in Joseph E. Holloway, ed. *Africanisms in American Culture*. Bloomington: Indiana University Press, 1990, pp. 185-210.

Meki Nzewi. *African Music: Theoretical Content and Creative Continuum: The Culture-Exponent's Definitions*. Hanns: Institut für Didaktik Populärer Musik, 1997.

Mello Moraes, Alexandre José de. *Festas e Tradições Populares do Brasil*. Rio de Janeiro: F. Briguiet, 1946.

Menezes, Bruno de. *Boi-Bumba: Auto Popular*. Belém: n.p., 1958.

Merriam, Alan P. *The Anthropology of Music*. 7th edition. Illinois: Northwestern University Press, 1978.

Meyer, Marlyse. "Le Merveilleux dans une Forme de Théatre Populaire Brésilien: le Bumba-meu-Boi." *Revue d'Histoire du Théatre*. (Janvier-Mars, 1963): 94-101.

_____. *Pireneus, Caiçaras: Da Commedia dell'arte ao Bumba-meu-Boi*. 2a. ed. Campinas: Editora da Universidade Estadual de Campinas, 1991.

Moraes, Joila. "O Bumba-meu-Boi de Axixá." *Revista Maranhense de Cultura*. Ano II, 2 (Janeiro-Junho de 1978): 35-36.

Moraes, Jomar. "Bumba-meu-Boi: Folguedo e Vitória do Povo Maranhense." *Projeção do Nordeste*. Ano II, 13 (Junho-Julho de 1981): 4-14.

Murphy, John Patrick. "Performing a Moral Vision: An Ethnography of Cavalo-Marinho, A Brazilian Musical Drama." Thesis (Ph.D.) Columbia University, 1994.

Nadel, S. *La Théorie de la Structure Sociale*. Paris: Les Editions Minuit, 1970.

Nketia, Joseph Hanson Kwabena. "African Roots of Music in the Americas: An African View." *Report of the 12th Congress, London, American Musicological Society* (1981): 82-88.

Nogueira, Antonio Francisco. *A Raça Negra sob o Ponto de Vista da Civilização da África*. Lisboa: Typografia Nova Minerva, 1880.

"O Boi." *A Tarde*. Ano I, 6 (2 de Julho de 1915) São Luis, Maranhão.

"O Boi." *O Globo*. Ano V, 1 (2 de Julho de 1858) São Luis, Maranhão.

O Estado do Maranhão. (9 de Junho de 1974; 5 de Agosto de 1977; 12 de Agosto de 1977; 17 de Maio de 1979;.10 de Junho de 1979) São Luis, Maranhão.

O Imparcial. (15 de Junho de 1861; 23 de Junho de 1976; 31 de Julho de 1977; 8 de Agosto de 1981) São Luis, Maranhão.

O Jornal. (27 de Abril de 1978) São Luis, Maranhão.

Oliveira, Ernesto Veiga de. *Instrumentos Musicais Populares Portugueses.* 2a. ed. Lisboa: Fundação Calouste . Gulbenkian, 1982.

Oliveira, Noe Mendes de. *Folclore Brasileiro: Piauí.* Rio de Janeiro: Fundação Nacional de Arte, 1977.

O Velho Brado do Amazonas. Ano I, 43 (27 de Setembro de 1850): 3.

"Pelo Desenho do Couro eu Sei se o Boi Vai Ganhar." *O Estado do Maranhão.* (30 de Junho de 1976).

Pereira, João Batista Borges. *Côr, Profissão e Mobilidade: O Negro e o Radio de São Paulo.* São Paulo: Editora da Universidade de São Paulo, 1967.

Pereira de Melo, Theodore Guilherme. *A Música no Brasil Desde os Tempos Coloniais até o Primeiro Decênio da República.* Rio de Janeiro: Imprensa Nacional, 1947.

Pierson, Donald. *Negros in Brazil, a Race Contact at Bahia.* Chicago: University of Chicago Press, 1942.

"Policia que Dá e Apanha." *A Tarde.* Ano I, 4 (30 de Junho de 1915) São Luis, Maranhão.

Prado Jr, Caio. *História Econômica do Brasil.* São Paulo: Editora Brasiliense, 1945.

Prado, Regina Paula dos Santos. "Todo Ano Tem: as Festas na Estrutura Social Camponesa." Dissertação de Mestrado, Universidade Federal do Rio de Janeiro, 1977.

Publicador Maranhense. Ano XXVIII, 131, (11 de Junho de 1869).

Queiroz, Maria Isaura Pereira de. "O Bumba-meu-Boi, Manifestação de Teatro Popular no Brasil." *O Campesinato Brasileiro.* Petrópolis: Editora Vozes, 1973.

Raffard, Henri. *A Indústria Sacarífera no Brasil.* Rio de Janeiro: Lombaerts, 1882.

Ramos, Arthur. *As Culturas Negras no Novo Mundo.* Rio de Janeiro: Civilização Brasileira, 1937.

_____. *As Culturas Negras no Novo Mundo.* São Paulo: Companhia Editorial Nacional. 3rd. Ed., 1979.

_____. *O Folclore Negro do Brasil.* Segunda Edição. Rio de Janeiro: Casa do Estudante Brasil, 1954.

_____. *O Negro Brasileiro*. Vol. 1, 2a. ed. São Paulo: Companhia Editora Nacional, 1940.

Redação. "Boi-de-Mamão Catarinense em Disco." *Boletim da Comissão Catarinense de Folclore*. Ano XVII, 32 (Novembro de 1979): 46-47.

Reis, José Ribamar Sousa dos. *Bumba-meu-Boi, o Maior Espetáculo Popular do Maranhão*. Recife: Editora Massangana, 1980.

_____. "Preto Velho e Bumba na Casa da Nâgo." *Jornal de Hoje*. (2 de Agosto de 1981).

Ribeiro, Jose. *Brasil no folclore*. Rio de Janeiro: Gráfica Editora Aurora, 1970.

Rocque, Carlos. *Antologia da Cultura Amazônica*. Vol. VI. Amada: Amazonia Edições Culturais, 1970.

Rodrigues, Nina. "Sobrevivências Totemicas: Festas Populares e Folk-Lore." *Africanos no Brasil*. Terceira Edição. São Paulo: Editora Nacional, 1945.

Romero, Silvio. *Folclore Brasileiro*. Rio de Janeiro: Olympio, 1954.

Rowland, Beryl. *Animals with Human Faces: A Guide to Animal Symbolism*. Knoxville: University of Tennessee Press, 1973.

Sacks, Harvey. "On the Analyzability of Stories by Children," in Gumperz, J.J. and Hymes, Dell, eds. *Directions in Sociolinguistics: The Ethnography of Communication*. New York: Holt, Rinehart and Winston, 1972, pp. 325-345.

Sacramento, João Domingos Perreira do. "Chronica Interna." *Semanário Maranhense*. Ano I, 45 (Julho de 1868): 7-8.

Santos, José de Jesus. *O Bumba-meu-Boi do Maranhão*. São Luis: Gráfica São Paulo, 1971.

Serra, Astolfo. *A Balaiada*. Rio de Janeiro: Bedeschi, 1946.

Silva, Carlos Benedito Rodrigues da. "Ritmos de Identidade: Mesticagens e Sincretismos na Cultura do Maranhão." Pontífica Universidade Catolica, Tese de Doutorado em Antropologia, 2002.

Silva, José Calasans Brandão da. *Folclore Geo-Histórico da Bahia e seu Reconcavo*. Rio de Janeiro: Campanha de Defesa do Folclore Brasileiro, 1972.

Silva, José Pinheiro da. "A Capitania da Baia." *Revista Portuguesa de História*. Tomo VIII (1959): 45-276; Tomo IX (1960): 211-245.

Simonsen, Roberto C. *História Econômica do Brasil 1500-1820*. 2 vols. São Paulo: Editora Nacional, 1937.

Smith, Grafton Elliot. *In the Beginning: The Origin of Civilization*. New York:

William Morrow and Company, 1928.

Soares, Doralecio. "O Boi de Mamão no Folclore Catarinense." *Aspectos do Folclore Catarinense*. Florianópolis: Imprensa Oficial do Estado, 1970. pp. 17-29.

Souza, José Ribeiro de. *Brasil no Folclore*. Rio de Janeiro: Gráfica Editora Aurora, 1970.

Taunay, Afonso de E. *História do Café no Brasil*. Vol. II. Rio de Janeiro: Departamento Nacional do Café, 1939.

Tracey, Hugh. "The Social Role of African Music." *African Affairs* 53, 210 (January 1954): 234-241.

Três Séculos de Iconografia da Música no Brasil. Rio de Janeiro: Biblioteca Nacional, 1974.

Valente, Waldemar. "O Bumba-meu-Boi Visto pelo Padre Carapuceiro." *Revista Pernambucana de Folclore*. (Maio-Agosto de 1976): 68-70.

Vasconcelos, Francisco. "O Bumba-meu-Boi em São Luis do Maranhão." *Itaytera Crato Instituto Cultural do Cariri*. no. 9 (1963-64): 35-4.

Vasconcellos, J. Leite de. *Tradições Populares de Portugal*. Porto: Livraria Portuguese de Clavel, 1882.

Verger, Pierre. *O Fumo da Bahia e o Tráfico dos Escravos do Golfo de Benim*. Salvador: Centro de Estudos Afro-Orientais, 1966.

Vianna, Helio. *História do Brasil*. Decimo-Segunda Edição. São Paulo: Melhoramentos, 1975.

Vieira, C. A. Angioletti. "Na Dança do Boi-de-Mamão." *Boletim da Comissão Catarinense de Folclore*. Ano XV, 29 (Dezembro de 1975): 47-48.

Vieira Filho, Domingos. "Bumba-meu-Boi do Maranhão." *Brasil Açucareiro*. XXXVI (LXXII, 2) Agosto de 1968: 102-103.

_____. *Folclore Brasileiro: Maranhão*. Rio de Janeiro: Fundação Nacional de Arte, 1977.

_____. "Folclore do Maranhão." *Revista Maranhense de Cultura*. Ano I, 1 (Janeiro-Junho de 1974): 45-62.

von Sydow, Carl Wilhelm. "Folktale Studies and Philology: Some Points of View," in Alan Dundes, ed. *The Study of Folklore*. Englewood Cliffs: Prentice-Hall, 1965, pp. 219-242.

SELECTED DISCOGRAPHY

Boizinho Incantado Sotaque Ilha. *Bailarino das Areias.* MCK Coml Repres. Fonográfica LTDA, C.G.C. 8/0001-00, 2000.

Naiva, Francisco. "Quando Anoitece." *Bumba-meu-Boi de Axixá.* Unacam Stereo LPU. 2/0018, Rio de Janeiro: Chanteder, 1986.

NOTES

CHAPTER 1

1. Maria Isaura Pereira de Queiroz. "O Bumba-meu-Boi, Manifestação de Teatro Popular no Brasil." *O Campesinato Brasileiro*. Petrópolis: Editora Vozes, 1973, 158–159.

2. Luís da Câmara Cascudo. "Bumba-meu-Boi," in *Dicionário do Folclore Brasileiro*, 2a. ed. Rio de Janeiro: Ministério da Educação e Cultura, Instituto Nacional do Livro, 1954, 618.

3. Michel Simon paraphrased in Luís Chaves. "'Bumba-meu-Boi'" do Brasil: '"Tourinhas'" de Portugal." *Ocidente*. LVI, 254 (Junho de 1959), 352.

4. Gastão de Bettencourt. *O Folclore no Brasil*. Salvador: Publicações da Universidade da Bahia, 1957, 125.

5. Luis Chaves, op. cit., 353.

6. Queiroz, op. cit., 157.

7. *O Globo*, julho 2 de 1858 quoted in Queiroz, op. cit., 158.

8. Arthur Ramos. *O Folclore Negro do Brasil*. Segunda Edição. Rio de Janeiro: Casa do Estudante Brasil, 1954, 115–116.

9. Arthur Ramos. *As Culturas Negras no Novo Mundo*. Rio de Janeiro: Civilização Brasileira, 1937, 365–366.

10. Domingos Vieira Filho. "Bumba-meu-Boi do Maranhão." *Brasil Açucareiro*. XXXVI (LXXII, 2) agosto de 1968, 102.

11. Ibid., 102–193.

12. Américo recorded at the roundtable debate, São Luís (Maranhão), July 7, 1986.

13. Américo at the roundtable debate, São Luis, July 7, 1986.

14. Cécio Valdelino recorded at the roundtable debate, São Luís (Maranhão), July 7, 1986.

15. Beryl Rowland. *Animals with Human Faces: A Guide to Animal Symbolism.* Knoxville: University of Tennessee Press, 1973, 130–131.

16. See José Alípio Goulart. *Brasil do Boi e do Couro.* Vols. I and II. Rio de Janeiro: Edições GRD, 1966.

17. Koster paraphrased in Roberto C. Simonsen. *História Económica do Brasil 1500–1820.* 2 vols. São Paulo: Editora Nacional, 1937, 229.

18. Caio Prado Jr. *História Económica do Brasil.* São Paulo: Editora Brasiliense, 1945, 75.

19. Pierre Verger. *O Fumo da Bahia e o Trafico dos Escravos do Golfo de Benim.* Salvador: Centro de Estudos Afro-Orientais, 1966, 13.

20. Ibid., 20.

21. Simonsen, op. cit., 230.

22. Ramos 1954, 95.

23. Mário de Andrade "As Danças Dramáticas do Brasil." *Boletim Latino-Americano de Música.* Ano VI, Tomo VI (abril de 1946), 80.

24. José Ribeiro de Souza. *Brasil no Folclore.* Rio de Janeiro: Gráfica Editora Aurora, 1970, 386.

25. Américo recorded at the roundtable debate, São Luís (Maranhão), July 7, 1986.

26. Kazadi wa Mukuna and Tiago de Oliveira Pinto. "The Study of African Musical Contribution to Latin America and the Caribbean: A Methodological Guideline." A paper developed in collaboration with the "Grupo de Trabajo—CIDEM." *The World of Music* 32, 3 (1990), 103.

27. Portia K. Maultsby. "Africanisms in African-American Music," in Joseph E. Holloway, ed. *Africanisms in American Culture.* Bloomington: Indiana University Press, 1990, 205. See also Kwabena Nketia, "African Roots of Music in the Americas: An African View," *Report of the 12th Congress, London, American Musicological Society* 1981, 82–88.

28. Américo recorded at the roundtable debate, São Luís (Maranhão), July 7, 1986.

29. Alan P. Merriam. *The Anthropology of Music.* 7th edition. Illinois: Northwestern University Press, 1978, 190.

30. Hugh Tracey. "The Social Role of African Music." *African Affairs* 53, 210 (January 1954), 237.

31. See Pereira (1967) and Mukuna (2000).

32. José de Jesus Santos. *O Bumba-meu-Boi do Maranhão*. São Luís: Gráfica São Paulo, 1971, 14.
33. Domingos Vieira Filho. "Folclore do Maranhão." *Revista Maranhense de Cultura*. Ano I, 1 (janeiro-junho de 1974), 60.
34. Cascudo, op. cit., 140.
35. Padre Lopes Gama. "A Estulotice do Bumba-meu-Boi." *O Carapuceiro* no. 2 (11 de janeiro de 1840).
36. Id.
37. Padre Lopes Gama, quoted in Luís da Câmara Cascudo. *Dicionário do Folclore Brasileiro*. 2nd. ed. Rio de Janeiro: Instituto Nacional do Livro Ministério da Educação e Cultura, 1962, 791.
38. Vieira Filho, 1974.
39. Ano I, no. 3, 1850; José Arthur Boiteux. *Águas Passadas*. 2a ed. Florianópolis: Livraria Central, 1932, 5–17.
40. Cascudo, op. cit., 124.
41. Hermilo Borba Filho. *Apresentação do Bumba-meu-Boi*. Recife: Imprensa Universitária, 1967, 19.
42. Ramos, 1954, 95.
43. Theodore Guilherme Pereira de Melo. *A Música no Brasil Desde os Tempos Coloniais até o Primeiro Decénio da República*. Rio de Janeiro: Imprensa Nacional, 1947, 60.
44. Pereira de Melo, op. cit., 60–64.
45. Cascudo, op. cit., 124–125.
46. Ibid., 126.
47. Oneyda Alvarenga. *Música Popular Brasileira*. Buenos Aires: Fundo de Cultura Económica, 1947, 30.
48. Alvarenga, op. cit., 37–38.
49. Ibid., 38.
50. Queiroz, op. cit., 158.
51. Borba Filho, op. cit., 19.
52. Cf. Oneyda Alvarenga 1947, 38.

CHAPTER II

1. Américo recorded at the roundtable debate, São Luis, July 7, 1986.
2. Field notes; Pindaré, July 1986. See also Regina de Paula Santos Prado 1977, 126.
3. Field notes, São Luis, July 1981.
4. Prado 1977, 130.
5. Joila Moraes 1978, 35.
6. *O Jornal*, April 27, 1978.
7. *O Estado do Maranhão*. June 9, 1974.
8. *O Estado do Maranhão*. June 9, 1974.
9. José Ribeiro de Souza 1970, 350.
10. Prado 1977, 119.

CHAPTER III

1. E. Galvão. "Boi Bumba: Versão do Baixo Amazonas." *Anhembi*. Vol. III, 8 (1951), 276–291. See also *Jornal Pequeno* (23 de junho de 1966).
2. Kazadi wa Mukuna. *Contribuição Bantu na Música Popular Brasileira: Perspectivas Etnomusicologicas*. São Paulo: Terceira Margem, 2000, 172. See also Gerhard Kubik. *Angolan Traits in Black Music, Games and Dances of Brazil: A Study of African Cultural Extension Overseas*. Lisboa: Junta de Investigações Científicas do Ultramar, 1979, 22–24.
3. Kazadi wa Mukuna. "Sotaques: Style and Ethnicity in a Brazilian Folk Drama," in *Music and Black Ethnicity: The Caribbean and South America*. Edited by Gérard H. Béhague. New Brunswick: Transaction Publishers, 1994, 216.
4. Compare with ibid., 225–240.
5. Cited in Núbia Marques. "Centros de Tradição e Cultura." *Revista Sergipana de Folclore*. Ano I, 1 (agosto de 1976), 19.
6. Kazadi wa Mukuna 1994, 217.
7. Wilberforce W. Echezona. *Nigerian Musical Instruments: A Definitive Catalogue*. Lansing: Apollo Publishers, 1981, 125.
8. For a detailed discussion of this instrument, see Kazadi wa Mukuna 2000,

179–224.

9. See Kubik 1979, Fig. 31, 32, 33, 34.
10. See Jean-Baptiste Debret. *Viagem Pitoresca e Histórica do Brasil*. São Paulo: Editora da Universidade de São Paulo, 1972.
11. Kazadi wa Mukuna 2000, 179–224, See also Ernesto Veiga de Oliveira. *Instrumentos Musicais Populares Portugueses*. 2a. ed. Lisboa: Fundação Calouste, Gulbenkian, 1982, 410.
12. Meki Nzewi. *African Music: Theoretical Content and Creative Continuum: The Culture-Exponent's Definitions*. Hanns: Institut für Didaktik Populärer Musik, 1997, 34–35.
13. Interviewed in São Luís (Maranhão), December 20, 1982.
14. Sérgio Figueiredo Ferretti, ed. *Tambor de Crioula: Ritual e Espetáculo*. São Luís: Serviço de Imprensa e Obras Gráficas do Estado, 1979, 44–48.
15. Jeovah Silva Franca. "O Meu Bumba-meu-Boi." *Cultura Popular* (julho de 1981), 47.
16. Cyro Falcão. *Bumba-meu-Boi do Maranhão*. São Luís: Universidade Federal do Maranhão, s.d., 19.
17. João Domingos Perreira do Sacramento. "Chronica Interna." *Semanário Maranhense*. Ano I, 45 (Julio de 1868), 7.
18. José de Jesus Santos. *O Bumba-meu-Boi do Maranhão*. São Luís: Gráfica São Paulo, 1971, 19.
19. Rocque 1970, 248.
20. Dulce Martins Lamas. "Boi-bumbá e Pássaros." *Revista Brasileira de Folclore*. Ano VIII, 20 (Janeiro/Abril de 1968), 38.
21. Gustavo Barroso. *Ao Som da Viola*. 2a. ed. Rio de Janeiro: Departamento de Imprensa Nacional, 1949, 221.
22. Alceu Maynard Araújo. *Cultura Popular Brasileira*. São Paulo: Melhoramentos, 1977, 59–60.
23. Cyro Falcão, op. cit., 1.
24. *Bumba-meu-Boi de Axixa*. Unacam Stereo LPU 2/0018, s.d.
25. See transcriptions. All songs are transcribed from *Bailarino das Areias* CD recorded in 2000 by the Boizinho Incantado troupe from São Luís (Maranhão). Other songs are selected and transcribed from field recordings as performed by the Boi de Zé Vale troupe in Pindaré.

26. Falcão, op. cit., 3.
27. Mário de Andrade. "As Danças Dramáticas do Brasil." *Boletim Latino Americano de Música*. Ano VI, Tomo VI (Abril de 1946), 73–74.
28. Canuto Santos quoted in O Imparcial, 8 de Agosto de 1981.
29. Nonnato Masson. "A Morte do Bumba-meu-Boi." *O Globo*. São Luís, 21 de Junho de 1955.
30. *O Estado do Maranhão*, 9 de Junho de 1974.
31. *O Imparcial*, 8 de Agosto de 1981.
32. *O Estado do Maranhão*, 17 de Maio de 1979.
33. Joila Moraes 1978, 35.
34. Falcão, op. cit., 2.
35. Id.
36. *O Estado do Maranhão*, 9 de Junho de 1974.
37. Santos, op. cit., 19.
38. Lamas, op. cit., 36.

CHAPTER IV

1. Kazadi wa Mukuna 2000, 225.
2. For further discussion on this theoretical application, see Kazadi wa Mukuna 2000, 225–228.
3. Souza, op. cit., 351.
4. Regina Paula dos Santos Prado. "Todo Ano Tem: As Festas na Estrutura Social amponesa." Dissertacao e Mestrado, Universidade Federal do Rio de Janeiro, 1977, 119.
5. Souza, op. cit., 350.
6. E. Galvão. "Boi Bumba: Versao do Baixo Amazonas." *Anhembi*. Vol. III, 8 (1951), 276.
7. *O Velho Brado do Amazonas*. Ano I, no. 43, 27 de Setembro de 1850.
8. Ibid. Ano I, no. 3, 3 de Julho de 1850.
9. *O Imparcial*, 15 de Junho de 1861.
10. *Samanário Maranhense*, 5 de Julho de 1868.

11. *Publicador Maranhense*, 9 de Julho de 1869.
12. Barroso 1949, 219.
13. *A Tarde*, 2 de Julho de 1915.
14. "A Morte de Bumba-meu-Boi." *O Globo*, 21 de Junho de 1915.
15. Ibid., 21 de Junho de 1955.
16. *O Imparcial*, 31 de Julho de 1977.
17. *O Imparcial*, 31 de Julho de 1977.
18. *O Estado do Maranhão*, 12 de Agosto de 1977.
19. Alan P. Merriam. *The Anthropology of Music.* 7th edition. Illinois: Northwestern University Press, 1978, 2.

CHAPTER V

1. José Vale, interviewed in Pindare, June 30, 1986.

www.ingramcontent.com/pod-product-compliance
Lightning Source LLC
Chambersburg PA
CBHW051538020426
42333CB00016B/1984